THEORY AND PRACTICE OF COMMUNITY EDUCATION

To
Happy Enyo, my loving daughter

THE THEORY AND PRACTICE OF COMMUNITY EDUCATION

A Comparative Study of Nordic, British, Canadian and Ghanaian Experiments

ALBERT D. K. AMEDZRO
*Senior Resident Tutor, Institute of Adult Education,
University of Ghana, Legon, Ghana*

GHANA UNIVERSITIES PRESS
2005

Published by
Ghana Universities Press
P. O. Box GP 4219
Accra, Ghana
Tel   233 021 513401, 513383, 513404
Fax   233 021 513402
e-mail: ghanauniversitiespress@yahoo.com

© Albert D. K. Amedzro, 2005
ISBN: 9964-3-0325-4

PRODUCED IN GHANA
Typeset by Ghana Universities Press, Accra
Printed by Yamens Press Limited, Accra

CONTENTS

Foreword ix
Acknowledgement xi

Chapter
1. THEORIES OF COMMUNITY EDUCATION 1
   Introduction 1
   The Concept of Community 1
   The Concept of Community Education 4
   A Typology of the Community Practice of Adult Education 5
   Scope of Community Education 7
   Models of Community Education 8
   Literacy and Community Education 9
   Approaches and Methods in Community Education 9
   Motivation in Community Education 13
   Conclusion 17

2. SOME PRACTICAL EXPERIMENTS AND RELATED THEORIES IN COMMUNITY EDUCATION: FROM THE DEVELOPED COUNTRIES 19
   Introduction 19
   The Folk High Schools in Nordic Countries 19
   The Antigonish Movement in Canada 25
   The New Communities Project in Leigh Park, Britain 31

3. THE AWUDOME INTEGRATED COMMUNITY EDUCATION PROGRAMME IN GHANA 40
   Introduction 40
   Awudome Traditional Area 40
   The Judiciary 41
   The Awudome Residential Community Education
      Programme 43
   The College, the Community and Social Development
      Programmes 50
   General Course Offerings at the Awudome Residential
      Adult College 58
   Kpodoga, The Rural Community Newspaper 63
   The Demonstration Farm, Tsawenu 72
   Emerging Issues 79

4. COMPARISON OF COMMUNITY EDUCATION
   EXPERIMENTS IN DENMARK, CANADA,
   BRITAIN AND GHANA   86
   Introduction   86
   Origins   86
   Theories of Community Education Used   87
   Model of Community Education Used   87
   Typology of Community Education Adopted   88
   Approaches and Methodologies   88
   Role of Animateurs/Community Educators   90
   Content and Context of Community Adult Education   91
   Conclusion   91

BIBLIOGRAPHY   *93*
Index   *97*

FOREWORD

The account of the four adult education institutions well presented in this book is, indeed, a saga which is, at one and the same time, romantic and realistic, as well as pointing to new vistas for adult education in Ghana and society generally.

It is a story that brings together experiences and practices from other countries, thus providing a basis for discussion on comparative adult education. The Nordic, the British and the Canadian experiences are all brought in as essential ingredients to complement the Ghanaian experience.

The Oxford Delegacy approach to liberal education may have started it all. But it was the acceptance of the concept of a residential college based on the Folk High School that really got things moving in Ghana. It was when the concept was embraced by the local élite of Tsito who was able to gain community support for it that desire was translated into action.

The action attracted support from the Department of Extra-Mural Studies of the University College of the Gold Coast, and through it, further material and financial support came from local and foreign organizations, including UNESCO.

The Adult College became a reality. It has since provided various and varied programmes: liberal education, professional education and ticket courses. It has opened its doors to other organizations and institutions to organize their own programmes.

Above all, the 'Adult College' has been an original and unique approach to African adult education, sponsored by the Institute of Adult Education of the University of Ghana. The addition of a rural newspaper, the *Kpodoga,* and a demonstration farm at Tsawenu to its programme offerings has meant that the University realizes that for the emerging society of Ghana, literacy and modernized agricultural methods and practices are essential growth points worthy of the attention of the academia.

Furthermore, it has to be observed that the people of Awudome, spearheaded by Tsito residents, have access to the College and especially to the assembly hall, which has become the community centre. This is as it should be. It is in recognition of the fact that the importance for the construction of the 'Adult College' originated from the Awudome community.

This carefully written book is commended for the attention of individuals and organizations, which are interested in community education and development. It is a book about the potentials of education for hope, development and survival.

E. A. HAIZEL
Former Director, Institute of Adult Education
University of Ghana, Legon

ACKNOWLEDGEMENT

I am grateful to Mr. R. A. Banibensu, Mr. Samuel Nsowah and Mr. Nat Ambra, all of the Institute of Adult Education who read the draft so many times through. My thanks also go to Miss Pauline Kumdah who spent much time to type the draft neatly.

I express my thanks sincerely to Mr. E. A. Haizel, a former Director of the Institute of Adult Education, for editing the draft, for making very useful suggestions, and also for writing the Foreword to the book.

I am greatly indebted to Mrs. Evelyn Appiah-Donyinah also of the Institute of Adult Education who did the proof-reading and editing. Her suggestions have been very useful in the final preparations of the draft book.

The author is very glad to express his warmest thanks to Mr. Yao Aduamah, the editor of *Kpodoga,* who made available some very relevant materials for discussion in this book.

ADKA

Chapter 1

THEORIES OF COMMUNITY EDUCATION

Introduction

Experience in the field has shown that many development projects in communities collapse because beneficiaries have not received the appropriate education to help them change their attitude to participate in projects. Achieving effective participation of communities in development activities depends largely on the theories of community education that the community worker adopts in the field. The concept of community and some theories of community education are, therefore, discussed as guides to the community educator.

The Concept of Community

The concept of community connotes different issues to many people. The most popular use of the concept refers to geographical location. In this sense, community refers to people living and working in a defined geographical location. Here, members develop relationships based on common concerns. They get nurtured and develop the spirit of togetherness, help one another and share common norms, beliefs and behaviour patterns. Togetherness enhances communion with one another, promotes virtue and social wholeness. Three main features, namely, a distinctive name, a recognizable dialect and a common boundary are noted.

Brookfield (1986) indicated that in the urban centres what is popularly developed is the neighbourhood community. It also has delineated geographical boundaries. However, relationships are impersonal. Where there is no neighbourhood community, the community educator creates one to be able to effectively work with the people.

The analysis of the concept of the community advanced by Brookfield (1986) is not different from that of the German sociologist Ferdinand Tonnies (1855–1936) (reported in Light, Keller and Calhoun, 1989). Tonnies describes the relationship in the traditional community or a small isolated village, the *Gemeinschaft*, as very cordial. In a *Gemeinschaft*, people share common lineage, are in constant contact even on daily basis and participate in many communal activities. The common descent, common norms and concerns bind them together socially and emotionally. Their roles are ascribed and their survival depends on the survival of the *Gemeinschaft*. They, therefore, attach themselves closely to it, live in it, defend it, and die in it.

Tonnies sees the relationship in the urban society, the *Gesellschaft*, very different from that of the *Gemeinschaft*. The population of the industrial *Gesellschaft* is heterogeneous. People come from different social backgrounds with a diversity of occupations and professions. They have different aspirations and relationships are not cordial but superficial. They are very mobile and make new friends in their new environments.

As pointed out by Brookfield (1986) and Light, Keller and Calhoun (1989), some sort of arrangements is made in the *Gesellschaft* to establish the traditional sense of community. Apart from the establishment of neighbourhood communities, different kinds of networks based on interest, sex, occupation and social activities are built.

Neighbourhood communities are characterized by plurality of ethnic, occupational, class and various interest groups. They are thus based on various social and occupational interests and are referred to as communities of interest. Community adult educators break such interest communities into two categories. These are the communities of function such as those of lawyers and doctors and communities of interest such as all types of social and ethnic groups. In the broader sense, therefore, institutions and groups with common interests and concerns constitute communities.

Like Tonnies, Emile Durkhein, a pioneering French sociologist (1858–1917) differentiated between relationships and nature of communities in both traditional and modern industrial societies. He is credited for his concept of social solidarity: the way by which people are knit together in both types of communities. According to Durkhein, social forces bind people together in any type of community. Durkhein mentions two basic forms of social solidarity:

1. Mechanical solidarity;
2. Organic solidarity.

Mechanical solidarity prevails in simple or traditional societies. Here, the sharing of common beliefs, values and customs and participation in simple activities bind people together. People in simple societies view themselves as the same people and conclude that they are alike. The view of belongingness unites them. Some of the activities they undertake together include the building of their own houses, production of their own food and making their own clothes. They hardly depend on others for the basic needs of life.

Durkhein views division of labour as the main tool that binds people together in modern industrial communities. The division of labour differentiates the simple from the industrial society. In the latter society, there exists a wide range of specialized jobs and services to satisfy the demands of members. Individuals have the opportunity for creativity and development. Social interaction among people is intensified because of the development in science, technology, transportation, the communication system and production of goods. Under the circumstances, people become highly interdependent. Each person depends on the services and goods of the other person. Durkhein observes that the social bonds created by the system become stronger than even in the mechanical solidarity systems. It is in view of this strong social solidarity in the modern society that Durkhein draws the analogy of a living organism to modern societies. The organism of a whole person is more important than his component parts. This is the origin of organic solidarity. Society is united together to satisfy members' needs as well as to avoid crime and condemn those who disrupt the system.

Bensman's (2001) analysis of community is not different from those discussed above. Bensman notes that, in sociological and anthropological terminology, the community refers to a relatively small, isolated centre with a stable population. All economic and social services are viable and sustainable. It is a traditional society and forms a coherent whole: a unified pattern. Social relations are primary, direct and impersonal. These relations are based on traditional values and mores and are reinforced by a rich traditional celebration to maintain peace, stability and continuity. Norms rather than legislations are the means of social control. There is no room for individual choice and rational decision-making. Roles based on age, gender, lineage and family positions are ascribed.

Bensman has explained that the ideal community emerges in the wake of modern industrial urban society. With the rise of modern society, traditional forms of the community have been destroyed and replaced by the mass society. It is against this background that voluntary communities or functional equivalents of the traditional isolated communities have emerged to give people the social and psychological benefits of the community. These are professional and occupational groups, neighbourhood, ethnic, social and political groups.

Bensman points out that the term community in a less technical sense, refers to groups of people who share the same values. They may be economic, social and political units, or hamlets, villages, towns and cities sharing the same values.

The six main features, which are essential elements to the community as noted by Hallenbeck *et al.* (1962), quoted in Brookfield, are people, place, common concerns, organization, morale and government. Briefly put, a community refers to a consciously identified population with common needs and aspirations. It may occupy a geographically defined area, engage in common activities and have some form of organization to make it possible for it to meet its common needs. The important factor for fostering these communities is, however, community education.

The Concept of Community Education

According to the United Nations Universal Declarations of Human Rights (1948), everybody has the right to education. From the cradle to the grave, human beings learn so as to develop and adjust to changes in one way or the other, in the community. Learning has thus become a very important strategy to survive.

People, therefore, continue to learn throughout life whether non-formally, formally or informally. They learn in schools and through the process of self-education in reading, travelling, discussion, watching and listening. One school of thought noted, however, that the effectiveness and quality of a self-directed learning throughout life cannot be ascertained. It is not supervised and evaluated and may, therefore, be disastrous. It is haphazard and does not follow any system. Education must be supported and taken in partnership with an external agent. It must be supervised and promote the spirit of inquisitiveness and acquisitiveness. In the words of Brookfield (1986), one main purpose of education is to inculcate the habit of independent learning skills in learners. But self-directed learning fails generally to build these skills and the learner can relax at any point of time for one reason or the other. People need some sort of organized education to help them adapt comfortably to situations but may not demand or get opportunities for it. It is then that community education must be made available to people to make them function effectively and efficiently.

Baba (1994) describes community education as all educational activities organized by or in collaboration with the community to meet its developmental needs. In the process, it utilizes available resources including its institutions. This makes community education cost-effective. An important feature of community education is the involvement of the community in determining the education activities relevant to its needs. It is a process of increasing the capacity of individuals to understand their reality. This will enable them to initiate appropriate actions to deal with socio-economic and political forces of oppression within the community to enhance personal and community development.

Community education is, therefore, a process in which views of the local people are tapped and with collective efforts educational activities are undertaken to respond to the concerns, expectations and needs of the people. Functional education is employed to capacitate communities to take part in the process of production, to document the processes of culture and to provide social avenues for personal and community development. It is, therefore, related to the prevailing circumstances in the locality. A friendly social and psychological education climate conducive to learning is created in which everyone naturally wishes to acquire literacy skills. Community education is to bring people together to help one another and in the process, help themselves. Experiential learning method, by which participants in the natural societal setting actively take part in the learning process to acquire and apply skills and knowledge immediately, is used. This mutual support leads to social change whereby communities work as a group rather than as individuals. It encourages the formation of social and voluntary groups for common goals as occupational co-operatives, women's groups and readers' clubs.

A necessary feature of community education is functional literacy, which embraces all fields of community life. Surprisingly, however, the most prevalent type of community education programmes in the developing countries are the official institution-based ones. In this type of community education, government officials of various departments initiate the programmes whether in health or agriculture. Their focus reflects government policies. Community values are somehow suppressed. As Freire (1972) notes, education should take place in a natural environment and should not be confined only to institutions with rigid top-down curriculum and administration to kill initiatives of people.

A Typology of the Community Practice of Adult Education

Brookfield (1986) has identified a typology of three main dimensions of community practice of adult education. These are (1) adult education for the community, (2) adult education in the community and (3) adult education of the community. None of them is, however, mutually exclusive.

Adult Education for the Community
Adult education for the community is the main type of education provided in the community. Adult educators would like to offer programmes which are relevant and of immediate use to the community. As a result, the adult educator depends heavily on the needs assessment of the community to draw his programmes.

Based upon the community's own identified felt needs, the educational programme is organized for them. This is the consumer-oriented or community-oriented type of adult education to satisfy the expressed needs of the community members. The educator plays an administrative role in the organization of a programme and appoints facilitators for it.

As with all needs assessments, a variety of needs may emerge. Some of the criteria for the prioritizing of these needs should include:

1. Availability of facilitators for the course;
2. Availability of funds and participants for the course;
3. The type and status of people selecting a particular course;
4. The educational value of a particular course to the community (Brookfield, 1986).

Adult Education in the Community
Adult education in the community is organized in the natural environment without the use of classroom facilities in the community. It is a typical non-formal education programmes which is organized outside the classroom. It is organized on farms, factories, under trees or at any convenient place. Both local human and natural resources are mobilized for the learning process.

The educator, however, provides other learning inputs to support the learning process as appropriate. Although the learners set their own goals for learning, the educator is a catalyst in the leaning process in offering professional advice. Community members are given the opportunity to develop their talents through independent, self-directed and self-planned learning.

Adult Education of the Community
Adult education of the community is more of the traditional formal type of education. The educator believes in the power of education as a tool for development. He is the master of his own subjects and possesses all essential information on education. He, therefore, adopts the banking approach in teaching adults.

The educator believes that the community must be equipped with leadership and problem-solving skills so that people will be able to develop themselves and the environment. He, therefore, knows and plans what to teach and how to teach it. The education process is thus educator-centred. In this sense the educator decides on what type of education to improve conditions in the environment.

Much emphasis is placed on the transmission of values to ensure the existence of conformity and the establishment of a healthy society. To all intents and purposes, the educator is determined to implement the educational or development plan he has envisaged for a community.

Scope of Community Education

Community education is a political tool used in community development to enhance social change and justice. The scope of community education is, therefore, wide and very comprehensive. It focuses on all aspects of life and activities available in the environment to alleviate poverty and promote sustainable development in the community. Community education is crucially important for agriculture and the occupations of people, health, literacy, water and sanitation, environmental improvement and the promotion of responsible citizenship.

Another important scope is in the area of culture. It is from this point that the concerns of the people would be easily identified and their interests aroused to embrace the development and education process. Generative themes would then reflect cultural lives of the people. It was for this reason that Freire set up study groups termed "culture circles" in communities to advance their culture as the base for the promotion of functional literacy. Cultural advancement of communities is then to promote the socio-economic development of communities. It is also from cultural perspectives that education could be used to respond to specific needs of people.

One major concern of modern community education is participation of women in community programmes. In many communities, there are many factors, which traditionally militate against women participation in community education and development activities. Women are usually relegated to the background and fall under a category of people who are victims of the 'culture of silence' as mentioned by Freire (1974).

Illo (1990) noted several interrelated factors, which hinder women's participation in community education. These include traditional role allocations, early marriages, restricted movement of women, the burden of multi-family roles and economic concerns. According to him, women are engaged in food processing, crop storage, water and fuel wood collection and marketing of variety of items including food items either processed or unprocessed. Other factors include inadequate education, information and taboo barriers. Men prescribe the roles and responsibilities of women. Women cannot take initiatives and even dare not ask questions. They remain in their ignorance and tend to find fault with themselves rather than the system, which puts them in that situation. Appiah and Cusack (1999: 25) sadly noted that "women are the weaker vessels in the community . . . so husbands deny them their freedom. Most married men do not want their wives to associate themselves with the rest of the people. So they insist and force them to stay in the house, while they go about doing what they like". Taboo barriers, isolation and traditional work overload also deny women the opportunity to actively take part in community education programmes.

Since the essence of community education is to mobilize all human and natural resources towards the development process, the focus of community education is on the silent majority, the women. They are homemakers, working in almost all aspects of traditional life while at the same time they are the first educators of families in the community. They, therefore, really need community education to make them function more effectively in the community.

Community education relates to equity by which individuals irrespective of age, sex, culture, class, race, religion, occupation or educational level benefit from the educational programme to fulfil themselves and society.

Community education is, however, not pursued in isolation. It is implemented within the national education and development framework. It is in view of above that Knowles (1970) explained that community education must be considered not in isolation but at three main levels: the individual, institutional and community levels.

Models of Community Education

According to Brookfield (1986) there are two major models of community adult education. These are the Liberal and Liberating models.

Liberal Model
The Liberal Model of Community Education is based on the premise that the community is a homogeneous entity where all people are equal and free and that they can be freer and more enlightened when exposed to education. A liberal education programme can, therefore, help communities identity and satisfy the needs of all members of the community at the same time. This form of education is provided by an agency concerned with the satisfaction of the needs of community members through social and educational programmes. Common education programmes to enlighten the horizons of members are, therefore, organized.

Liberating Model
The Liberating Model of Community Education is based on the assumptions

that there are structural injustices in society as mentioned by Freire (1974). Injustices exist in the political, social and economic spheres of the community. A small group of members hold fast to power to the detriment of the majority. The former monopolizes economic, political and social powers. It is through radical education that these inequalities are eliminated to promote collective well being of members. The essence of this model of education, radical in content and approach, is to raise the consciousness of members to take action and bring social and political change.

Literacy and Community Education

As mentioned earlier, literacy is a necessary tool in the community education process. One might argue that community development can take place without literacy and that local illiterate farmers can produce crops for the market; that they could improve their yields through the use of extension officers; that through experience on the farm they could produce more. But experience takes a long time to acquire. Bad practices might even be adopted in the course of experience gathering. Experiences might be obsolete in the modern era. If however, the market economy improves, if the economy becomes more complex, if the market becomes competitive and the demands for globalization should be met, literacy becomes a necessity. Literacy can accelerate community education so that the farmer can organize his business, learn new methods of production, access markets and capital and improve upon his lifestyle. As Bhola (1979) explained, literacy is a social capital which can be utilized by communities and individuals for their own and national development.

Kassam (1982) realizing the importance of literacy in community education advocates a simultaneous integration of literacy skills and vocational training on intensive and selective basis to enhance community development. He argues that even though social development can take place without literacy, literacy can accelerate its progress. Freire (1974) notes that through literacy people will be able to read, record and calculate their daily transactions. People will be able to read about others and communicate with their neighbours. The consciousness of literate communities will be aroused to know the realities of life. They will then take action to liberate themselves from the shackles of injustice and build a just society.

Approaches and Methods in Community Education

The diversity of communities and complexity of their educational needs have demanded a multi-facet approach to community education. One of the important initial strategies is to identify and train local leaders. This is because community members can easily accept local leaders since both live together and know local conditions and cultures. These leaders must be trained by the community educators to develop their moral and intellectual ability. They must acquire leadership skills to mobilize the community and inspire them to learn. These qualities will enable them to build a strong team spirit among community members to promote individual and community performance. This core of leaders will continue to monitor the progress of the programme even if the community educators should finally withdraw.

Another appropriate strategy is the formation of study and discussion groups as Freire (1974) recommended. These leaders can establish small groups of readers and radio listening groups and interest groups as appropriate. In small groups, adults will actively participate in the learning process.

It is also important to know and work with traditional structures that exist in the community. As noted by Ampene in Bown and Tomori (1979: 45).

> It is important for the adult educator to know the existing structure or arrangements in his area of operation since the traditional culture is still a living entity and the majority of West African people can best be reached with adult education programmes that follow traditional channels or structures of communication.

Ampene was referring to traditional structures in West Africa. But this scenario applies generally to structures in communities in general. These structures will disseminate information faster and also support community education programmes. It is also important to collaborate with both national and international structures with similar orientations so as to pool resources together for effective community education.

In the presentation of packaged learning methods, a variety of methods must be adopted to satisfy various tastes. These may include lectures to introduce new ideas and concepts. Platforms may also be created to promote discussions among the people as Freire mentioned and practised.

The use of community newspapers and readers' clubs also promotes and sustains community interest in learning. These papers prevent learners from relapsing into illiteracy and always keep them in the literacy tune (Amedzro, 2001).

Amedzro (2001: 30) mentioned other methods, which are applicable in the delivery of packaged community education materials. These include games, counselling, group work and activity methods. In the activity method, learners undertake activities such as drawing, dancing and singing not only to apply theories to solve problems but also to keep all participants actively involved in learning activities. Other methods include seminars, demonstration and workshops, open forums, games and fieldwork. The rest includes simulation such as role-playing, drama, stories and proverbs.

Community Entry Approach: Participatory Rural Appraisal
Education in any form does not just occur. It is started by people to solve a problem or to reflect policy goal. In order to achieve the best of results in any of these ventures, it is necessary to identify the issues involved. The identification could be done through an appropriate research method, which must start, with the community entry approach.

Community entry approach is the initial and continuous contact and interaction of development officers with community leaders and members to create awareness among the people on the need for education and development. It is to solicit their interest and make the programme acceptable, participatory and sustainable. It is also to meet community's identified needs. It is when these felt needs are addressed that communities will accept the programme. This will also enhance the community sense of belonging and ownership of the programme. An added advantage is that communities identify themselves with the programme and see themselves as co-workers and so will not let it collapse. Participatory Rural Appraisal is one of the major techniques in community entry approach.

Until recently, the traditional research method whereby the elite collect data in the field without much involvement of the local people in the exercise is used. This method as Pratt and Loizos (1992: 8) noted was "perceived by local groups as intrusive, aggressive and distanced and that too much development planning has been a top-down affair, carried out in the name of local welfare but over the heads of local people". It is against this background that community education is preceded by participatory research.

According to Pratt and Loizos (1982), the most appropriate research package for any community education and development work is the Participatory Rural Appraisal (PRA) method. Tools of PRA include Transect Walk, group and focus group discussions. These are supported with film shows and publicity activities available. Initially, community educators as appropriate, observe traditional protocol. Local political structures are identified and robed into the education campaign. The main objectives of the exercise are well explained to the local people.

The PRA is a team activity, which involves the experts and the various groups in the community. It is thus a control against personal biases of the experts. It demands of the experts to spend some time in the community and take part in their activities so as to identify themselves with the local people. The local people must get to know and accept the community workers and *vice versa*. As the experts stay with local people, the latter at times make mistakes as they take part in the work the local people do. The inferiority complex existing among the local people is broken. Confidence builds up as status differences are temporarily suspended.

Through the use of common instruments in the collection and analysis of data, both development officers and locals develop common interests and build common developmental aspirations.

An important aspect of PRA is the visualization of village productivity or problem to the locals. This can be achieved through the discussions of community map, calendars (rainfall seasons, crops) matrices comparing two or more variables and diagrammes such as the Venn Diagram or the tree which are produced at the end of the transect walk. Through these discussions, locals visualize the level of their education and development and the need to undertake some other development or educational programmes. The locals become more developmentally focused as they prioritize their development needs and tasks. Discussion groups are formed to identify resources, find out causes of their problems and suggest solutions to them. The discussions are held under the non-directive guidance of community development officers.

Participatory Rural Appraisal can be used not only to arouse the awareness of locals to undertake development projects which they come out with during the discussions. It can also be used as a mediation tool to solve community management problems, land disputes and resource utilization problems.

In many cases, a variety of needs arise during discussions. All the needs cannot be tackled together. One way of eliminating other needs is by casualty exercise. A certain need may lead to the occurrence of others. Its eradication may necessitate the eradication of others too until the main need is arrived at. This process of arriving at the main need is what Freire (1974) refers to as, the conscientization process. From baseline studies, according to Freire (1974), participants are taken through the word register of words collected. Through discussions generative themes (self-needs) are arrived at. It is at this point that functional literacy begins.

The community need is important but the community workers can suggest a need to the people. This should be handled in a subtle manner. The best of results can be achieved if the community workers hold a series of informal sessions with the community before the formal discussions are held.

Publicity materials such as handbills, T-shirts, logos, adverts and posters could be used to prepare the minds of people towards the discussions. These will ensure that the need gains prominence in the minds of the local people and prepares them to formulate it clearly. Community workers must, however, structure the project in such a way that when it is started, other needs mentioned by the people will be satisfied.

Participatory Rural Appraisal is a useful research package, which can mobilize communities to gather meaningful information to create the awareness and need for change. Such information is owned by the people and, therefore, accepted by them. It helps communities to identity their strengths and weaknesses and helps them prioritize, plan and implement their development activities in the political, economic and social and educational fields as appropriate. Participatory Rural Appraisal followed by relevant education generates a positive feeling of self-reliance and empowerment of all those involved.

Motivation in Community Education

Adults in the community are saddled with very many commitments and are, therefore, no "captive audience" in the learning process. In many cases, communities initially and at times in the course of community education programmes may be handicapped to take active part in the programme.

Motivation is a very important factor in community education. It is defined by Fowler and Fowler (1973) simply as "what induces a person to act". Here, motivation is related to learning and is, therefore, defined as factors that induce people to learn.

According to Rae (1994), motivation is an internally generated attitude and learners join the learning programme with a range of motivational attitudes and at various levels. Some may register against their wishes because of community pressure. They may want to save their faces. Some may not see the need for learning because of their age. They may advance psychological, social and physiological reasons. These may include financial, health, housing, occupational, extended family and marriage problems. They may also be afraid of failure. Others may think that they already know what the programme is going to teach them since they have been able to survive with the methods they adopt over the years.

In the discussion of motivation, one fundamental issue that must keep on emerging is that members must feel the need for requisite knowledge. People, especially adults in the communities, need education but might not ask for it. It is against this background that motivation in community education is paramount.

What the development officer needs to do is to encourage them to motivate themselves. It is logical for the officer to give a local and acceptable explanation about how the learners will benefit from the new skills, how they will grow as a result of the experience and their chances of progressing in their chosen careers. These must be explained against the background of technological and social changes, as well as the competitive environment and organizational changes.

Meaningful motivation provided regularly goes a long way to elevate the motivational levels of learners to enhance performance and helps in the attainment of community education and other forms of education and training objectives. The Incentive Theory of Motivation in community education is important.

This theory is concerned with the pattern of behaviour that is biologically determined. The theory proposes areas like the desire to reduce drives or to maintain an optimum level of arousal. Motivation in this sense is externally induced.

Human beings are thus presumed to have natural drive to survive. The course of survival can then be directed through education. People in any environment, therefore, have the natural drive to have the requisite knowledge, skills and attitudes needed for development. The tendency is then to welcome any learning process that will enable them to achieve their ambition. It is the responsibility of the development officers to provide relevant education.

Cognitive theories of motivation focus on the role of our thoughts, expectation and understanding of the world. The basis of cognitive theories lies in the fact that people believe certain behaviours can make them realize their goals. Thus, by organizing and reorganizing their perceptions on issues or problems, they will get what they want. In applying this to education, the assumption is that because of the perceived rewards that go with acquisition of knowledge to enhance one's status, skills, competence and even promotion and work, people tend to participate in educational programmes. The level of motivation, however, depends largely on how the cognitive objectives have been achieved (Feldman, 1996). The goal of achieving these can be well directed by the community educator.

There is yet another motivation theory, which deals with feelings and human nature. This is McGregor's Theory of Management, explained in Hope and Timmel (1984), which he called Theory X and Theory Y. Theory X notes that:

1. The average person is by nature lazy and will not put in much effort to achieve result.

2. The average person lacks ambition, dislikes responsibilities and prefers to be led.
3. The average person is inherently self-centred, indifferent to organizational needs and goals.
4. The average person is by nature, resistant to change.
5. The average person is not very bright and can easily be led by a dictator.

Generally speaking, this theory connotes that many people inherently dislike work and study and must, therefore, be coerced, controlled, given instructions and supervised to achieve community or organizational goals. The community educator must study the situation and supervise the learning process with care to appropriately direct the course of learning.

On the other hand, Theory Y believes that the individual by nature has the capacity, ability and motivation to meet the aims and objectives of the community. He has the capacity to exercise self-direction and self-control to achieve objectives to which he is committed.

While the implementation of Theory X in the educational process is likened to Paulo Freire's banking concept of education, the Theory Y is synonymous with the liberating education process. By the latter, participants are taken into partnership in the learning process. Teamwork is promoted and the principles of delegation and developing the human resources are supreme in the education process. Thus, syndicate exercises and fieldwork promote learning and bring out the best of the participants. Such techniques build the initiative of participants and improve their performance. All that participants require is encouragement and opportunities to perform well.

Another important theory on motivation in the educational process is that linked to Maslow's hierarchy of human needs. Maslow's model proposes different motivational needs hierarchically organized. Maslow's (1968) thesis is that the satisfaction of certain primary human needs motivate individuals to function well in the community. These needs which Maslow believes must be satisfied from lower level to the upper level are physiological, safety, social, esteem and self-actualization. His contention is that the satisfaction of one need leads to the satisfaction of the higher need till all the needs are satisfied.

The satisfaction of these needs to motivate one to participate in learning or the development process is very important. However, the satisfaction of the needs in order from the lower to higher needs may not necessarily follow although the satisfaction of basic needs is important. The fact, however, remains that these needs must be satisfied to motivate people and promote the happiness and participation of individuals in the development process. Maslow (1968) however, omits one fundamental need, which is the need to learn so as to help one to know and adjust oneself to changes around. It is at this juncture that Rogers (1959) noted the important role the individual plays as an intervening variable in exerting some influence in the learning process. It is the responsibility of the facilitator to provide the opportunity and create the environment for people to be motivated to satisfy their needs. The nature of needs would determine the nature of issues people should learn and how they must be taught. All educators must find ways and means of motivating people to strive towards self-actualization.

Some of the features of motivation raised by this theory are drive, stimulation, arousals and activation which move people to either perform an act or refrain from it. Keeping adults to be aware of their progress is a way of reinforcing motivation. The performance of people in any educational programme is usually linked to the individual ability and his level of motivation. A well-developed community education programme should embrace the needs of the beneficiary, assess their motivational levels and have an integrated evaluation process built into the programme.

It must be emphasised that adults enter educational activities with specific problems, which reflect the social roles they perform. Motivation for learning varies according to individual interests because of their different needs. Community educators, therefore, need to study individual interests to provide the appropriate motivational techniques. This is what Freire (1974) refers to as situational approach but not subject approach on motivation. This was the origin of dialogical theory of Freire when he relied on need identification resulting in the formulation of generative themes. When generative themes are addressed, individuals are motivated to learn.

In brief, motivation in community education is very important for various reasons. Usually community members may not be aware about the need for education. Even those who may be aware may not ask for it. Also people who are disappointed once in an education are not excited the second time. They might not return without substantial encouragement. For these reasons, many motivational techniques should be applied to ensure continuous participation. Techniques could include all or some of the methods listed below to arouse and maintain the learner's interests.

1. Display of notices and news items on boards so that learners can write their own news items, short stories, proverbs and short sentences for other students to read;
2. Meetings to be made more interesting through narrating personal experiences;

3. Regular rallies and durbars on the importance of community education;
4. Educative entertainment such as drama, dances, theatre, poetry recitals and puppetry to attract people to learning;
5. Formation of study circles;
6. Use of posters;
7. Organization of participants for games such as *aware* and ludo.
8. Film shows;
9. Visits to people in their homes and in hospitals;
10. Open, prize-giving and community education days;
11. Exercises;
12. Provision of reinforcers: Comments about the learner's good work are social reinforcers. Affirmation and acceptance enhance approval motivation. They can make the learner and the community educator feel proud. Symbolic reinforcers such as good grades are also helpful. Tangible reinforcers including the distribution of badges, seedlings, pencils and pens to members with good attendance records serve as support. Tangible benefits in the form of material benefits from their work or organizations become the basis for acquisitiveness motivation. People are inspired to achieve more success through hard work. Activity reinforcers, in the form of a promotion to group leader, can also be used. Internal reinforcers, such as reading a good student's work aloud in class and narrating the achievements of a member are other important motivational activities. Curiosity motivation such as opportunities for continuing education and job placement for new members to be exposed to new stimuli, helps them to concentrate more on participation (Amedzro, 1994).

Conclusion

Community education is a process by which members of a community identify their needs and problems, live and work together to solve these problems.

The essence is that it is only through collective action that individual problems can be solved to improve their lives. In the process, individuals as well as the community become self-actualized: their needs are fulfilled.

Community education is not merely an adult education school in the community to offer counselling services and courses for adults. It has some specific attributes which include the following:

1. It starts from the cultural base of the people.
2. It is organized in partnership with the community.
3. It democratizes the decision-making process in education.
4. It identifies and finds solution to the needs of the community.
5. It utilizes all available resources for the common good of community members.
6. It adopts a variety of approaches and strategies to deliver learning materials.
7. It offers a variety of programmes to suit different interest groups in the community.
8. It promotes lifelong education.
9. It equips members with occupational and life skills (cultural, recreational and political).
10. It promotes participation through motivation.

Community education is a concept and the community school or an extension department is the delivery system. It is to gain the ground, which the formal school system has lost. Advocates of community education both in Britain, Canada and Denmark in the 1930s and later in the developing countries like Ghana in the 1950s adopted the Antigonish and Folk Schools as models of community education. Examples of these early community education programmes, some initiated by university departments in communities, are used as case studies in this book, illustrating the various theories and strategies of community education.

Chapter 2

SOME PRACTICAL EXPERIMENTS AND RELATED THEORIES IN COMMUNITY EDUCATION: FROM THE DEVELOPED COUNTRIES

Introduction

Many countries have embarked on the implementation of community education programmes but fail to reach the majority of the people. And this has happened in spite of the fact that one of the basic principles of community education is popular participation. The University of St. Francis Xavier in Canada and the University of Southampton in Britain also have adopted their own strategies to reach the people to get involved in community education. They are, of course, not alone in this venture but they are used as examples with which to compare the situation in developing countries like Ghana.

This chapter, therefore, attempts to identity some common problems and relevant theories concerning the application of community adult education. In order to do this, the chapter examines and discusses some practical experiments in Antigonish in Nova Scotia, Canada and Leigh Park in Britain; programmes designed specifically by university community education organizations to solve particular problems of whole communities or problems affecting certain groups of the population.

The Folk High Schools in Nordic Countries

Introduction
It has already been noted that, in some cases, community schools have been established to promote community education. Community members are to be brought into residence to take part in educational programme so that they can actively take part in the development process. Examples of such schools are drawn from the Nordic countries and Ghana in the proceeding chapters. Much attention is given to the situation in Ghana to illustrate how a developing country can make use of community school to promote education in the environment.

Origins of Residential Community Education
The residential community education idea originated from the Nordic countries, namely, Denmark, Finland, Iceland, Norway and Sweden (in

alphabetical order) in the early 19th century when the industrial revolution was in progress in Europe. Surprisingly, however, the economy of these Nordic countries was rather on the verge of collapse. The wind of the industrial revolution was slow to blow over them. The enterprising mid-level personnel who could start the industrial revolution were conspicuously non-available (Dam, 1986).

This was also the time for the rise of nationalism. But the Nordic countries could not boast to be nation-states. The people were divided among themselves and could not forge any strong common front to face outside influence. There was, for instance, a strong German pressure in the southern part of Denmark in the wake of German unification. The Danish King, Frederik VI was the duke in Slesvig-Holstein. The latter state earlier on belonged to Germany and Germany was fighting to recapture it in 1848–50 and again in 1864. These wars had consequences for the Nordic countries. There was instability. Property and lives were lost. The economy was collapsing. Holstein was lost to Germany in the end. There were also civil revolutions and religious revivals all over Europe challenging the absolute rule of monarchs and dogmatism of the Church (Andresen, 1992).

It was against these backgrounds that a new educational system was to be evolved to get adults involved immediately in the rescue operations. The person who has the credit for this educational innovation was Nikolaj Frederik Severin Grundtvig.

Innovation in residential community education was to combat the declining trend of the economy, relieve the people of their hardships, and arouse the sense of nationalism among them. These could be done through organized functional and residential literacy programmes.

N. F. S. Grundtvig (1783–1872), a theologian by profession, was a poet, philosopher, hymn-writer, historian, education reformer, politician and master of languages both 'living and dead' (Dam, 1986). As a clergyman, he was very much concerned with the welfare of his people. His concern was the provision of a meaningful education for the common man to make him realize his potentials. National institutions for the people were to be built to provide education for all. According to Grundtvig, the Soro Academy was to be transformed into a National Academy for People. He was always on the side of the poor. As a politician, he wanted to build national unity and identity among the Nordic people.

As an educational reformer, he advocated a pedagogical innovation which could allow for participation to equip beneficiaries with skills which would support them to make a living. He did not believe in compulsory education. Schools were to be free, enjoyable and natural. His Folk High

School idea was highlighted in his publication — *The Danish Four-leaf Clover-of Danishness Seen from a Partisan View.* Grundtvig's sermons, songs, writings and speeches then aroused the consciousness of people to participate in social and community development programmes.

A very laudable outcome of his chain reaction activities he set in motion was the agricultural co-operative movement. Soon each district formed its own movement to produce food and materials for its consumption and market requirements.

The three study trips made by Grundtvig to England had far-reaching effects on his thinking. His studies at the Trinity College in Cambridge, especially, convinced him that learning should be a participatory process. He was impressed by the lively interaction among learners and teachers in the classroom and the comradeship outside the classroom. This situation contrasted very strikingly with what prevailed in the University of Copenhagen where the social interaction among lecturers and students was poor (Andresen, 1992).

Grundtvig's conviction of participatory learning made him to formulate and popularize the idea of Folk High Schools. Grundtvig saw the need for these Schools to prepare people for participation in social affairs. This was to be done in such a way as to take its starting point and its material from the language, history and individuality of the Danish people (Dam, 1986). These schools were to be built by the rural people themselves. Grundtvig stated that education should be a 'school for life.', and be lifelong.

This view on education as lifelong to equip adults with skills to make life meaningful has been echoed by modern adult educators like Bown and Tomori (1979) and Nyerere (1976). It is necessary that adults update their knowledge, skills and sensitivity so that they will be able to improve upon their lives and contribute to community and national development.

The "people's university", according to Grundtving, was to bring the farmers, workers and theoreticians together and bridge the gap between the elité and the common man. It should help the individual take responsibility over himself and others.

The school system, which Grundtvig advocated, should be residential for adults. Folk (common people) High Schools, which were residential, were to be built to provide short courses in local affairs and vocations for adults. In these Folk High Schools, the ordinary man and woman were to be actively engaged in the educational process so that individuals could identify their own problems and solve them. At least, they could make a meaning out of their lives. The Schools were to stimulate and motivate local community to promote development and to make people interested in their affairs.

Grundtvig remained an educational reformer and philosopher and never established any of the Folk High Schools himself. His ideas, however, caught up with those of other educators who successfully experimented the Folk High School idea.

The history of the actual establishment of Folk High Schools started on November 7, 1844 when the first school with 20 farmhands were admitted to the school at Rodding in Denmark where German pressure was great. The German unification process threatened the annexation of parts of Slesvig and Holstein. The goals of the Folk High Schools were summarized in a speech read by the Principal, Johan Wegener at the ceremony marking the opening of the school:

> The young person shall here learn to think, speak and write clearly and soundly, sensibly and rightly. His heart must be instilled with love of his country, its language, its history, its ways and customs and establishments, so as to be made aware both of his nation's virtues and of its faults.
>
> Without this, the soul is neither moulded nor the mind improved. Without this, the peasant can never stand independent in the community. Without this, he will be dependent on everybody, and will on every occasion have to resort to their help, even though they are his enemies, and although he knows that they are (Dam, 1986).

The main objectives of the schools are, therefore, to train and produce people who must know their culture, love their country and acquire skills to make meaning out of their lives.

Many earlier Folk High Schools had been established in Denmark. But the most popular one, which has an everlasting history and has made its mark for posterity was the one established by Christen Kold (1816–70) in 1851. Kold enrolled the common people from the local community in his private school. He experimented the home-like environment in the school. Both facilitators and participants led a common life. He came down to the level of participants and talked with them in a simple manner. The participants successfully learnt their local history. Some learnt one skill or the other while others improved upon their vocational skills. His experiment was most successful and news about it spread far and wide. The Folk High Schools then sprang up throughout the Nordic countries.

Lectures and discussions were not the only media of instruction in the schools. Singing became a very powerful vehicle of education. Grundtvig, himself a popular hymn-writer, wrote many songs. The contents of the songs were also discussed with the people. Soon, songbooks written for the schools were circulated to other sectors of the society. Tunes and songs suitable for particular occasions were composed and sung in almost all homes in the country.

A special Danish musical tradition was then established. Great names associated with this tradition were Severin Grundtvig, Carl Nielsen and Thomas Laub.

The importance of the Folk High Schools cannot be underestimated. The schools were able to arouse, nourish and clarify a higher regard for human life in general and for the human-life of the Danish people and the Danish man in particular "than one usually meets with" (Dam 1986). The self-confidence of the rural population was built. The schools were also able to stimulate the national consciousness of the people. Youth clubs, open lectures, community singing, lecture societies, all organized by the schools were eye openers to people's participation in local and national affairs.

The contribution of graduates of the Folk High School towards the economic and social development of Denmark was also great. These graduates formed different types of associations to undertake social development activities. The agricultural co-operative movement from the Folk High Schools was able to mobilize people for the production of raw materials and foodstuff. All over Denmark, former pupils or teachers of Folk High Schools are members of local government councils, parliament and different types of organizations. Their contributions to their communities have been noteworthy (Dam, 1986).

Main Features of A Folk High School

The main characteristics of the Folk High School are that they are independent of government control in terms of the curriculum. The curriculum of each school, drawn by students and teachers, is to satisfy local conditions and participants' needs. Local history, the crafts and agriculture are some of the subjects handled. Lessons are conducted in local languages for the benefit of all to participate actively.

The schools are small institutions and are residential. The size of the schools is to make room for more social interaction among participants and also strengthen participant-facilitator relations. They are built in the rural areas and are named after the communities in which they are. They have close relationship with the communities in which they are built. The local people take part in open educational programmes like lectures, debates and festive evenings. A closer relationship is built between the schools and the community since local people are always appointed board members. Andresen (1992) mentioned some other characteristics of Folk High Schools:

1. Students come mainly from rural areas.

2. There are long winter School for young-men and a shorter summer school for young girls.

3. There are no examinations of the school. The schools are to transmit Life-Enlightenment, concentrating on the human being in Denmark and his contribution to his society.

4. Christianity was introduced as a subject in the first generation Folk High Schools. Both Christians and non-Christians are however, admitted at the schools.

5. The schools are to create national consciousness and cultural richness so that students should "become free, courageous, and conscientious citizens".

6. They are all boarding schools bringing students and teachers together to share temporarily, a close and mutually responsible fellowship.

In 1870, there were 52 Folk High Schools. In 1880, and in 1890 there were 64 and 75 schools respectively. This shows that there was an increase of at least 11 schools in a decade from 1870 to 1890. But the mushrooming of the schools slowed down for almost a century (from 1890 to 1980) when the number picked up again.

In 1980 they were 80 and were about 100 in 1991. It was estimated that an average of 10 per cent of the youth in the twenty-year old bracket participates in courses at the Folk High Schools. It meant the schools appealed to that age bracket (Andresen, 1992). The national or state Folk High Schools envisaged and propagated by Grundtvig have, however, never been established. The schools remain community schools.

Curriculum Design

There are two main types of courses run at the schools. These are the short courses which last for one or two weeks and the long courses which last mainly between two and six months. In the long courses, project-oriented classes or school line-up subjects were pursued. Students learn subjects in depth. In the short course programmes, the programmes are tailor-made to suit age groups or occupational groups. The programme is tight and learners get busy all the time. It is organized for more mature adults. Each school is responsible for the development of its own curriculum. Both students and teachers plan the curriculum and method of teaching which include the combination of theory and practical work, work in small study circles, lectures, workshops and student-managed classes.

Folk High Schools are noted for their extra-curricula activities. These include participation of both learners and facilitators in common meetings, morning assemblies, community meals, community singing, sporting activities, bike trips, midnight discussions, and school parties with entertainment and music. Many Folk High Schools publish their own music books depicting their culture. Briefly put, the schools are open to all citizens irrespective of sex, religion or political beliefs. But the emphasis is on the common man. People join them voluntarily to improve upon their standards and develop their communities (Andresen, 1992).

The Spread of Folk High Schools
Folk High School models were established in other countries in Europe in the later part of the 19th century. In Britain, they are known as Residential Adult Colleges. The most notable of these colleges in Britain is the Fircroft College at Birmingham, while that in Canada is the Antigonish Institute which started in 1921 with 51 unusual group of students made up of working men from all walks of life and especially, farmers (Laidlaw, 1961).

Conclusion
The formal residential community education idea formulated by Grundtvig materialized in the Nordic countries in the second half of the 19th century in the establishment of Folk High Schools. These are community educational institutions which equip members with skills to participate in the community development process. The schools are mainly community schools. Their curriculum reflects the social and occupational aspirations of communities.

The Antigonish Movement in Canada

Introduction
The St. Francis Xavier University in Canada started one of the earliest community education movements at Antigonish. This university is a Catholic University, which developed from a Grammar School. Because of its Christian religious foundations, it has been greatly concerned with the welfare of people. Like the University itself, the University Alumni Association kept close contact with community members and participated actively in her activities. The University has, therefore, not adopted the traditional attitude of many universities which have kept their distance from the 'market places' (Laidlaw, 1961). It has not developed the traditional university attitude merely to train leaders for the future generation. As Laidlaw (1961) put it, the community education movement was not primarily an institution 'to combat intellectual poverty', but

rather sprang from 'the desire to combat poverty in the material things of life' (Laidlaw, 1961). It was aimed at improving the economic and social conditions of farmers, fishermen and workers in general.

Towards the end of the 19th century and particularly at the beginning of the 20th century, Nova Scotia began to suffer more severe economic hardships than other parts of Canada. There was a great urban drift of people, which led to the decline of agricultural activities. The population of the Antigonish county, for instance, was reduced from 18,060 in 1831 to 10,073 in 1931. Laidlaw (1961) noted that 'the decade 1921–31 was the most calamitous, when whole districts lost as many as half their population in a veritable flight from the land'.

Conditions became unbearable after the First World War when economic recession set in. The three main industries, namely, farming, fisheries and mining suffered heavy setbacks. The fishing industry at Canso was seriously affected. Fishermen became extremely poor and desperate. Unlike the farmers who deserted their farms when farming became unrewarding, the fishermen had no choice but to remain in their settlements. Those who could find jobs were those who had to work for the rich men living in the area. Unemployment and frustration set in for the majority. Poverty became real for the majority of residents. It was against this background that St. Francis Xavier University started its community education programme with headquarters at Antigonish in the University to help the suffering inhabitants.

The Early Moves Made by the University to Help the People
One of the earliest pioneers of the Antigonish Movement was Dr. Hugh MacPherson. In addition to his normal lectureship in the Department of Agriculture, he managed the college farm and started an extension work with the farmers. His main aim was to encourage the establishment of co-operatives among workers. He organized the farmers into the formation of co-operatives, taught them the importance and application of fertilizer, the treatment and sale of wool and sheep. He organized the sheep farmers into co-operatives. He arranged meetings with them on the improvement of their occupation and lives. The co-operative members were taught how to wash their wool, keep it clean, roll and tie it. They were not allowed to sell them untreated at very low prices. All the wool produced by the members was collected at one point. With a collective bargain, they were able to get a better price for their fleece. Instead of 17 cents per pound, they sold their fleece for 28 cents. They were now an organized group, learnt to improve upon their wool production and get a better deal. It was the beginning of the producer co-operative movement of the Antigonish fame. The foundations for the extension service have thus been laid. This was in 1914.

Some Practical Experiments and Related Theories 27

This was a very bold and good attempt made by MacPherson to organize the people into co-operatives. They might have been aware of the need for the formation of co-operatives. They might not have got the initiative or a facilitator among them. The community educator provided them with the opportunity to organize themselves into a functional community education group.

At the time, Dr. Jimmy Tompkins was the Vice-President in the University. Tompkins' idea was also similar to that of MacPherson — to use community education to improve the conditions of the people. While MacPherson was concerned more with the farmers' welfare, Father Tompkins was interested in general education for the larger community. Both worked together to promote the ideals of the Antigonish Movement.

In January 1921, the latter brought 'an unusual group of 51 students (Laidlaw, 1961) to undertake community education programme on the University campus for two months. It was made up of working men from all walks of life. This was the beginning of the 'People's School'. In the following year, 60 participants were registered in the People's School at Antigonish. Two other sessions were held at Glace Bay, in the industrial area of Cape Breton. The main subjects discussed were English Language, Economics, Public Speaking, Mathematics and Agriculture (Laidlaw, 1961). Tompkins' determination was "to bridge the gap between book learning and real life, and to put knowledge into a form that ordinary people could understand and use (Lotz, 1977: 105 quoted in Brookfield: 1986). He was transferred from the University on pastoral duties in 1923 and continued his community education work with fishermen at Little Dover and helped them to establish their own cannery. He organized classes for them and provided them with study materials (Brookfield, 1986). The dreams of Tompkins had materialized when in 1928 the extension department was established by the University with the appointment of his nephew Father Moses Coady as its Director.

The attempts and sacrifices made by the pioneers of this extension department were laudable. They used their leisure to work with the people to help themselves. They did not only send the University to the people: Tompkins brought them to the University. The education given them had elements of their profession in it — agriculture. It was not purely an "Oxbridge" type of liberal studies but radical liberated form of community education.

The Extension Department Moved into Action

In 1930, Father Coady visited a number of centres engaged in extension services in Canada and the USA and MacDonald his assistant toured western Canada to get themselves acquainted with adult education programmes. When they came back, they started work immediately. They did not wait for the people to invite them before they extended educational opportunities to them. As Father Coady stated, they went more than half way to meet the people since they believed that the people needed education but might not ask for it (Laidlaw, 1961).

This was a very important step taken by the community adult educators. They went to the people and established cordial relations with them before the formal programmes started. It was a practical way of opening the 'ivory gates' of the University of St. Francis Xavier to the ordinary people in the community.

Approaches and Methods

The initial methods they usually adopted to arouse people's interest in educational programmes were mass public meetings. One or two extension professors in a speech or speeches, outlined the problems facing individuals and the society. They always pointed out that if they utilized the opportunities available, they could overcome their difficulties.

The people's consciousness was then aroused through the speech of the professor who was conversant with individual and local problems such as family worries, bad weather, poor harvest or economic hardships. These he illustrated in his speech suggesting how they could be resolved together. In explaining his strategy in dealing with communities, Coady wrote that "intellectual dynamite would be exploded at this meeting and that an intellectual bombing operation would serve to blast those minds into some real thinking" (in Brookfield, 1986).

This top-down approach to development when development issues are raised by the community workers but not by the people, was applicable in the 1930s. Coady, for instance, built all ideas of development around himself "using intellectual dynamite to bomb people's mind", as he himself stated.

But in the 1960s, community adult educators like Paulo Freire challenged this approach to development. They advocated and practised the bottom-up approach to development whereby the initiative for introducing the generative themes or issues relating to the lives and occupations of the people should emerge from the people themselves. They were to identify, discuss and find solutions to their own problems. In Freire's conscientization method (Freire, 1974) more subtle method is to be used through the discussion of generative themes such as landlord, plough and farms introduced by the clientele. This method builds confidence in the clientele for identifying and discussing their own issues. In both cases, study groups were used. The groups in the former method were known as the Study Clubs while those in the latter were Culture Circles.

Study Clubs

By 1934, there were 932 Study Clubs in Nova Scotia. Brookfield intimated that by the year 1939, 19,600 people in the United Maritime Fishermen's Union were registered in 2,265 Study Clubs and 342 credit unions were in existence. It was through these Study Clubs that the Extension Department carried out its work. These clubs like the Culture Circles of Paulo Freire could be favourably compared to the People's Educational Association (PEA) of Ghana. It is through the PEA that the Institute of Adult Education University of Ghana carries out its extension programmes. In Antigonish, there were also radio listening groups, which discussed radio broadcasts on relevant local issues as it is done in Tanzania.

Leadership Training

Leadership courses were also organized by the extension department in Antigonish for communities. In January 1933, the first short leadership course for the Study Clubs was run at the University. Eighty-five participants were drawn from all over the country for a six week course. The evaluation report on the course was that,

> . . . it has been found that since they (participants) returned to their respective communities they have assumed the responsibility of leadership in the way of organizing more Study Clubs and taking the lead in all worthwhile community activities (Laidlaw, 1961).

Training of leaders and of those who will in turn train them has become an annual feature of the Extension Department of the University of St. Francis Xavier. A community newspaper, *The Extension Bulletin,* and a library with travelling library services were also started to educate the people and provide reading materials for them.

The methods used generally were organized mass meetings, study groups, discussion circles, training courses, kitchen meetings, community and refresher courses. As a result, communities were able to access funds from the banks to finance their economic activities.

Strengths and Weaknesses of the Antigonish Movement

The Antigonish Movement has its advantages and disadvantages. The educational programmes, as defined by the University, were related to the needs of the people. A practical example was demonstrated on active participation in co-operatives and credit unions. The wretched farmers and fishermen began to sell their own produce and exported some of them. Their conditions and environment improved. Laidlaw (1961) pointed out that between

1926 and 1955, personal incomes of these people increased by 94 per cent in real terms in the Maritimes. He went on to say that the co-operative groups in the three Maritime Provinces — Nova Scotia, New Brunswick and Prince Edward Island became large 'business organizations with an annual turnover of more than $52,000,000 in marketing and consumer supplies only' (Laidlaw, 1961: 122).

They also had about $30,000,000 in savings. These were great achievements since the poor low-income workers had no previous financial stand. They were also able to enjoy insurance and credit schemes, benefits, which were before then, not known to them.

In the field of community adult education, the Antigonish Movement has successfully raised the consciousness of the people to solve their own problems. They could read and write and reckon figures. The movement emphasized group learning and action. Workers have learnt to bargain collectively.

The University of St. Francis Xavier was brought closer to the people. Laidlaw (1961) stated that representatives of the fishermen, coal-miners and steelworkers were board members or governors of the University. He pointed out also that some outstanding leaders of the workers were awarded honorary degrees. Members of the Study Clubs registered as members of the alumni association and attended alumni meetings. All these were done to arouse and sustain people's interest in education and in involving them in the activities of the University.

The Movement, however, had its problems and failures. Laidlaw (1961) mentioned that initially, many of the communities accepted the philosophy of the movement with enthusiasm. This enthusiasm waned in some circles. The extension programme could not sufficiently mobilize the people in these areas. Laidlaw, however, did not specify those communities which 'have fallen back again into a state of lethargy and backwardness' (Laidlaw, 1961). He did not give the actual reasons for their falling back into that state. Could it have been that the programmes were imposed on them and that they were not given the chance to identify their own needs?

There was no attempt made to organize some of the workers who also needed help. Too much attention was paid to the organization of the fishermen and food growers. Laidlaw pointed out that nothing was done to organize and help the producers of lumbering and forest products. No help was extended to the pulpwood and Christmas tree cultivators, the two important farming groups in Brunswick and Nova Scotia. This should not have happened because adult education organizations must not discriminate against any type of profession or any group of people. Discrimination in Antigonish might not be intentional.

Some Practical Experiments and Related Theories 31

One other problem with Coady's educational programme as Thompson (1980) pointed out, was that when Coady died in 1959, he literally carried away with him the dynamism of the Movement. The problem of charismatic leadership in community education is noted. Coady's ideas were, however, institutionalized into the establishment of the Coady International Institute.

Conclusion

This section attempts to discuss some of the strategies adopted, largely by a university community adult education organization in Antigonish to mobilize the people for community improvement and employment. It has been discussed that human needs are many and varied. An attempt by the community adult education organization to mobilize the people for community improvement took various needs of the people into consideration. Work through local institutions, collaboration and regular contacts with clients are necessary and essential preconditions for sustaining their morale. There is also the need for use of existing structures and the creation of new ones. The most important element in the success of the community adult education programmes, however, is dedication on the part of community educators. In the case of the Antigonish programme, Thompson (1980) drew the conclusion that, "Despite its limitations it (the Antigonish Movement) is still a good example of how such work can be developed from a committed adult education base."

This conclusion is very relevant for the purpose of this study. It rightly points out the fact that when adult education organizations are committed to their work, problems of development would be sufficiently tackled. The Antigonish Movement solved the problems of participation in community improvement and employment. The credits for these were due to the dedication of the educators and the involvement of the people in the programmes to solve their problems.

The New Communities Project in Leigh Park, Britain

Introduction

Leigh Park is a large housing estate in Hampshire used as an overspill area for Portsmouth in Britain. The chief account of this experiment is given by Fordham, *et al.* (1979).

As a result of inadequate housing during the first half of the 20th century, and the second world war damages in Portsmouth, Leigh Park was developed outside the city in the 1970s. The Portsmouth City Council at Leigh Park started a special estate development programme from 1948. It was to rehouse families, which were rendered homeless by the German bombardment of

Portsmouth, when Portsmouth was a British naval base for the war operations. Leigh Park has by then become a settlement of some 40,000 people but initially, lacking in many social amenities. It lacked adequate transport facilities and job opportunities. Entertainment and entertainment centres were non-existent. Many of the residents faced severe economic problems because of lack of job opportunities (Fordham *et al.*, 1979).

At the beginning of the New Communities Project of the University of Southampton in 1973, the residents of this estate seemed not to be interested in any development activities in the area. It is at this juncture that there exists a corresponding behaviour between residents of and conditions in Leigh Park and those in the developing countries. There existed despondency to development programmes. The residents of Leigh Park, especially the youth, became restless. They even went to the extent of destroying property. The middle class, who could afford it, bought their own houses in the adjacent areas. The inhabitants seemed to know little about their immediate neighbours. Fordham and his colleagues (1979) pointed out how unfavourable the people of Havant Borough Council and the Portsmouth City Council seemed to neglect the residents of Leigh Park once the latter were provided with the estate houses.

It was against this background that the New Communities Project Team, a community education organization, was formed in Leigh Park. This team was,

> to observe and examine the attitudes of residents and professional educators towards adult education provision as it existed in 1974 and if necessary, to develop more relevant approaches (Fordham *et al.*, 1979: 4).

What this study sets to find out is how a community education association, the New Communities Project Team, was able to arouse the residents' interest to participate in programmes to improve upon the community. The strategies for mobilization and motivation to awaken the people out of their despondency and sustain their interest in local activities are relevant to the purpose of this study. These strategies can be adopted to suit conditions in the development of communities in developing countries.

The Leigh Park experiment has its own shortcomings. On the whole, however, it offers some useful illustrations in the mobilization of despondent people to improve upon their conditions as will be shown in this section.

The New Communities Project Team Moves into Action
The Project was a collaborative work planned by education organizations

such as the University of Southampton, the Workers Educational Association (WEA), the Local Education Authority and the Department of Education and Science, all of Britain. The project team was initially made up of two research fellows and later joined by a secretary and many volunteers.

The first strategy adopted by the community education association was to enhance the development aspirations of participants. For this reason, therefore, the project team went into the estate in early 1973 for this three-year action research programme. Amazingly, however, they moved into the estate without any prior information, discussion or consultation with the residents. Not even the residents' political representatives were informed about the intention of this adult education organization.

Fordham *et al.* (1979), however, gave the excuse that "in Leigh Park the local residents' groups have in the past effectively blocked other more traditional research proposals". It was for this reason that the team adopted an initial low profile strategy. But they failed to explain why the residents blocked earlier traditional research proposals. Could it have been that the residents did not accept the research topics? Or was it because the earlier researchers did not establish any cordial rapport with the residents? Or was it because the purposes of the traditional research proposals were not well explained? Or could it have been that the residents were never interested in any research work in Leigh Park? One is left to wonder why the residents protested against earlier research proposals. The project team did not attempt to find the answer. They only went in to develop the people. But this was a false start because as Julius Nyerere (1976) stated, no one can develop people. It is the people who must develop themselves.

As a result of the lack of establishment of an earlier rapport, the going was at first difficult. It was after the team had moved in and started work that it began to find ways and means of establishing rapport with the residents. Thus, while the team had to start actual business, it rather had to begin a probation period as the air was full of suspicion for the aims of the team.

The Breakthrough Strategy
The team then had to reorganize its strategies to build relationships with the local political administrators and the Labour Group. With time and tact, however, cordial relations were established between the two groups when the project team explained their objectives to them. It was after about six months of informal dialogue and negotiation that sufficient rapport was established with the people and community improvement programmes started. For example, work with the local playground movement led to the building of an adventure playground, which could cater for 200 children. Subsequently, the team became

a catalyst in the estate in many development programmes as well as liberal education classes and literacy classes, which were organized for the adult population.

The team realized that it was necessary not only to establish rapport with clients but also very important to give them the opportunity to participate in the decision-making process. They must be encouraged to identity themselves with the programmes. It was also appropriate to give publicity to the on-going programmes. This would not only arouse their interest but also maintain it. It was for these reasons that the 'Breakthrough Strategy' — the publicity drive — was launched by the project team to publicize their work.

After the initial six months' operation, the team got well established in the estate and felt able to launch the 'Breakthrough Strategy'. It was not only to publicize existing adult education programmes but also to discover more needs of the local people and attempt to find solutions to them.

The University staff for the campaign used a borrowed van. During the publicity week, the van operated at the shopping centres, public houses, factory gates and public places. The University of Southampton really came down from its ivory towers to meet the people at the common places. The project team distributed leaflets at these centres. It gave information and advice on how to fill questionnaires on what they would like provided or improved in the estate. Publicity also took the form of street theatre and performance by a pop group; the local radio and the press were brought in. People's curiosity was thus aroused on local issues and on what they could learn or do. In all, over 4,000 leaflets had been distributed. The process was a successful one in mobilizing the people for local development. As a result of these campaigns, day-release and vocational courses were also organized.

The points made so far are that, through these campaigns a community education organization was able to mobilize the people to look for ways and means of improving their communities. There was no need to acquire sophisticated materials for these campaigns. An old van, which was borrowed, was effectively used to communicate the messages around. People were given the chance to participate in identifying their needs and finding solutions to them. It was a good way of motivating them to take interest in community development. What was then necessary was to establish programmes serving the particular local needs identified. One of these was better communication about local problems and, for this and other reasons, the Team started a local community newspaper.

The Use of Community Newspaper
One other important way of motivating and sustaining the interest of the people

Some Practical Experiments and Related Theories 35

was through the publication of a community newspaper. *Leap,* the Leigh Park community magazine, was then launched and used by the Project Team. Among other things *Lead* was,

> to improve publicity for local events and organizations. To encourage and foster new groups, new activities and initiatives. To provide a vehicle for the drive of expression of public opinion. To provide information on important local issues so that people can better understand and influence decisions which affect their lives: where necessary to campaign for the rights of local residents. Its aim is . . . to provide a service to the 40,000 inhabitants of the area known as Leigh Park (Fordham *et al.,* 1979).

Action Groups and Common Forums
Besides the newspaper, the Project Team organized public meetings and groups to plan action on various issues. The objective of the community education organizations was to create forums for the residents to raise and discuss their issues and programmes. Fordham *et al.* (1979) illustrated how the Project Team helped the residents with, among other things, public transport, contact with officials and planning together specific projects like the Holiday Play Scheme. Through this scheme, people demonstrated their commitment to the community through good will, advice and help. They used school buildings, youth clubs and church premises to host meetings and programme activities. Through all these various groups, many for the first time, learnt to participate in the proceedings and operations of organizations. They participated in the discussion of political issues, the structure and operation of the Council which was responsible for the provision of their needs. They were now able to understand their environment better and become aware of where to get financial aid and other kinds of help. The illiterates were provided with the opportunity to participate in both basic and functional literacy programmes. Literacy materials and libraries were provided to encourage people to learn.

Through these meetings at the residents' leisure period and in holidays, community members were able to understand the forces under which they lived. The scheme was a successful education forum which brought the people together for local development programmes. They relaxed and discussed issues dispassionately and found answers to questions they raised. From this experiment, it is illustrated how adult education organizations should not impose their decisions and programmes on their clients. They should make room for their clients to discuss other issues in addition to those programmes introduced by the community agency.

The Use of Structures and Networks
In Leigh Park, the Project Team, after realizing its faults of lack of initial

rapport with the people, started to work with and through existing structures. Some of these structures were the Single Parent Family Group, which held discussions about health, child care, personal experiences and coping with a sense of loss; the Breakthrough Organization which was concerned with publicity; the Working Men's Group, the Deaf Club and the Holiday Play Scheme, all promoting their members' interests. Some residents belonged to more than one structure. The existence of these structures facilitated the easy spread of ideas from one structure to another. Thus, there was a constant contact between the Team and the residents through these networks.

The team realized that it was not sufficient to work with local structures only. It co-operated with external or other institutions/networks, which would give the necessary support and materials which local organizations, could not provide. In Leigh Park, community educators worked with networks such as the British Association of Settlements, the Home Office, and the Havant Borough Council. Without these outside networks, the Project Team would have found it difficult to work successfully single-handedly. It is in view of the importance of structures in tackling central issues successfully that UNESCO recommended that,

> Member States (of UNESCO) should endeavour to ensure the establishment and development of a network of bodies meeting the needs of adult education; this network should be sufficiently flexible to meet the various personal and social situations and their evolution (Quoted in Bown and Tomori, 1979: 279)

The Role and Significance of Animateurs

One other characteristic of the Leigh Park experiment which is worthy of note is the role of the animateurs — members of the Project Team and the volunteers. In the second year of the life of the project, 1974, there was the concern among the residents on the future operations of the programmes if the animateurs should leave. An important question then in Leigh Park was: what would be the fate of the project after 1975? There was also the need to validate the gains of the Project Team.

In December 1974, therefore, the first of the meetings among the three principal organizations involved in the project — the Department of Adult Education of Southampton University, the Workers' Educational Association (WEA) and the Local Education Authority took place to consider this issue. One of the important decisions taken was to incorporate the programmes into the regular structure of community education in the area. The organizations involved in the programmes were also to pool their resources together to supplement local efforts to run the programmes. New activities were

Some Practical Experiments and Related Theories 37

programmed. Some of these new developments included workshops for children and parents. The Leigh Park branch of the WEA was also formed. The local volunteers and the local branch of the WEA took responsibility over the administration of the project in the event of the final withdrawal of the Project Team. They were sufficiently prepared to take over this responsibility.

Creation of a Resource Centre
To facilitate the administrative work of the Project Team and also provide a resource centre to attract and give more educational opportunities to community members, the Leigh Park community acquired 230 Dunsbury Way. This building was given the catchy name 'Focus 230'. In a co-operative effort, all the networks and organizations in the community, helped by the organizational ability of the animateurs, rehabilitated this building. The Job Creation Scheme (a short-term device of central government to help solve youth unemployment) which was responsible for its rehabilitation saw to its decoration and furnishing for educational and entertainment programmes. The centre was open to any individual or groups as a resource centre for development. Such individuals could organize programmes there.

It was used as an advisory centre for people who needed any sort of advice or help. For example, it could be on the settlement of rent arrears or health needs. There was also a Children's Play Centre attached to it. Manpower and Job Creation officials were appointed to advise or direct the unemployed who consulted the centre on the issue of employment. A Holiday Committee was also formed to draw a constitution for the running of the centre. This committee with WEA members took over the responsibilities of the team when it withdrew. A teacher was appointed as a Warden for the building during the phasing out period of the Project Team. Members of the Holiday Committee and the Warden then closely worked with the team in its last three months. It was a programme organized to give the new organizers the chance to understudy the work of the animateurs. Residents assumed greater responsibility over their affairs. As a result of these developments, there was a wider publicity about activities at 'Focus 230' and it has become a focal meeting centre for many social and occupational groups in Leigh Park.

Programme Monitoring at the Official End of Programme
One of the greatest criticisms of the Leigh Park experiment, however, is the almost complete withdrawal of the University of Southampton from work in Leigh Park. There has been no formal link again with the centre by this organization. The excuse was that the exercise was an experimental one. This is a dangerous position in adult education when the adult education

organization withdraws completely and no follow-up programmes have been organized. The programme might collapse or the intended objectives be neglected.

Rogers and Shoemaker (1971) pointing out the importance of formal contacts and follow-up programmes used the case studies of Tappan and Wheeler (1943) to illustrate their point. This was the Home Canning Campaign in Georgia, USA in the early 1940s. Several hundred families were involved in this programme. They were supported in the canning programme with loans from the Farm Security Administration. The officials of this government agency used education to introduce the new ideas on canning of different kinds of food among families. The programme was to help poor women to be self-sufficient in a variety of the canned food. It was also meant to help them have the balance diet necessary for human growth. The production target for each family was 500 quarts. At the end of the fourth year when the programme came to an end, Lula, one of the women who at first was not prepared to take part in the programme, was able to can over 800 quarts. Her willingness to participate in the canning industry was finally due to the education given her by members of her peer group on the importance of the canning programme. Instead of using the canned food for meals, however, Lula kept them on the shelves to advertise her achievements.

Other women came to attach great importance to the mere number of canned foods they produced and preserved. Many of the families instead of making use of the canned food, displayed their food jars in the parlour, guest room or on the shelves in the kitchen after the project period had elapsed. There was little improvement in the economic and nutritional condition of the individuals because they had not yet adopted the idea that they should also consume the food they had canned. They developed objectives different from those set by the community educators.

Conclusion
This chapter discussed some of the theories and community education practices in three countries of the developed world. The focus was on Denmark, Canada and Britain. Two of the experiments were initiated by university dons to involve communities in the development process, while one was inspired by a nationalist for the same purpose. The three experiments, through innovative practices, were planned and executed in partnership with community members. The experiments had their weaknesses but managed to survive. Community members including some despondent residents participated and acquired occupational and life skills to effectively participate in the development process.

All the programmes aimed at responding to the immediate needs of communities they served. The commitment of the educators, the collaboration with other structures and enthusiasm of participants accounted for the success of these community education programmes.

Chapter 3

THE AWUDOME INTEGRATED COMMUNITY EDUCATION PROGRAMME IN GHANA

Introduction

In the mid 20th century, the Folk High School idea was extended to the developing countries. The establishment of these schools was a feature of developmental strategies in the wake of political independence. The schools were to prepare local people to participate in the development process. Such schools became popular institutions in Tanzania and were known as Folk Development Colleges. In Kenya, they are known as the Village Polytechnics. In Ghana, the only successful college built on the Folk High School model is the Awudome Residential Adult College (ARAC) at Tsito. The ARAC in Ghana antedates the Folk Development Colleges in Tanzania and the Village Polytechnics in Kenya.

Awudome Traditional Area

Introduction
Awudome Traditional Area in which this study took place is 140 km northeast of Accra. It forms part of the Ho District in the Volta Region of Ghana. It is divided into seven settlements. These are Anyirawase, Avenui, Bame, Dafor, Kwanta, Tsibu and Tsito (in alphabetical order) with some farming villages dotted all over the traditional area. Two of the towns, Dafor and Tsibu, are located west of the Ewe ranges on the Peki-Kpeve road. The others are on the eastern part of the range between Juapong-Ho and Juapong-Anfoeta roads. The traditional seat of government for the Awudome state is Anyirawase. Tsawenu where the Institute of Adult Education has a demonstration farm is a sub-village of Anyirawase.

Traditional Political Organization
Among the settlements, a definite degree of seniority is recognized, which does not depend on wealth or size of the settlement, but on historical events. According to traditional folklore, although the Avenui were in the vanguard leading the ancestors in their migrations and wanderings, the Anyirawase group of the people provided two persons to sacrifice to the gods. The ancestors, therefore, made a pact to let Anyirawase have the paramount stool.

The head chiefs of all the seven towns, upon their election as chiefs, swear the oath of allegiance to the paramount chief at Anyirawase. The climax of the yam festival, the most popular cultural festival in the traditional area, takes place at Anyirawase with all the seven divisional chiefs in attendance to pay homage to the paramount chief.

Avenui is the spiritual home of Awudome. At Avenui resides the spirit of the earth god called Mianor Zodzia (or Mother Earth). Like the paramount chief at Anyirawase, the priest of the earth god occupies an enormously central position in the Awudome Traditional Area. No community might begin to sow, harvest or eat yams until the priest at Avenui had performed the necessary customs.

Kwanta is the settlement where the Awudome warriors celebrate military victories. It was here that the Awudome people took off in order to build their various towns hence the name Kwanta meaning the junction or the parting place.

Tsito with a considerable population is the largest of the Awudome settlements. It is situated near the source of a permanent river. In the 1984 Population Census, it was one of the three towns in the Ho District with a population over 5,000 people. Despite its size and population, it is constitutionally recognized as one of the youngest settlements in Awudome (Asem, 1982). Tsito, according to oral tradition, was originally meant to be a military post to check enemy advances from the south.

At meetings, members are arranged in order of rank and seniority. The chiefs of Avenui, Kwanta and Bame occupy positions on the paramount chief's right. The chief of Tsito sits on the paramount chief's left. The chief of Tsibu sits behind the paramount chief while the chief of Daffor sits in front of him.

The Judiciary

The people have ways of reacting to wrong doings. People, especially women and children, may sing songs to ridicule thieves. The towns are divided into clans. Offenses are reported to the clan heads. Under no circumstances can a member of a clan take a case to another clan for arbitration. Offences are judged at the clan, village and town levels from where appeals can be taken to the paramount chief. Thus, Anyirawase serves as the supreme court of the area.

There are four types of offences, which are dealt with by the courts. They are:

1. Common or domestic types of offences such as theft or non-compliance to join in communal labour. These are taken to the judgment of clan heads or chiefs.

2. Trespasses against acknowledged laws of decency, respect or reverence of womanhood (*gudodo*). These include having sex in the bush, having sex with one's own very close blood relative, or breaking a taboo. These are judged by the priest of the earth god.

3. Criminal cases such as the intention to commit suicide, murder as well as land disputes are judged by the chiefs.

4. Divine Judgment or Trial by Ordeal: A person may be accused of causing death by means of witchcraft or sorcery. If the person pleads guilty, he is taken to the dunghill where his head is shaven and other customs are performed to exorcise him of his evil powers. However, if at the trial the person denies the allegation the Council of Chiefs will send him to undergo the ordeal of *Afakaka* (divination) to discover the truth by divine judgment. This is referred to in modern law as trial by ordeal. The judgment reached by a diviner is final. The punishment of a murderer includes his banishment from the community or demolition of his house or replacement of the murdered person with a number of living persons.

Religious Beliefs and Practices
There is a guardian god called *Dente* whose shrine can be seen at the entrance of every Awudome town. It prevents evil spirits from entering the town. There are also the earth god, *Mianor Zodzia,* a mountain god called *Eveto,* two river gods known as *Wuve* and *Tsawe.* Wednesday and Fridays are kept sacred for *Eveto*. On these days, no one may go to work in the fields. Everyone must be at home on market days too. No community might begin to sow, harvest or eat new yams until the priest of the earth god at Avenui has poured libation and offered prayers to his god.

The annual yam festival and unlucky portents as droughts or epidemic diseases also provide occasions for the priest of the earth god to cleanse the community of evil spirits. Cleansing the community of evil spirits is known as *Dumekpokplo* or *Dubabla.*

Many customs are, however, not performed today because of the influence of Christianity and formal education while the central government enacts laws such as the law against trial by ordeal to practically change "unsatisfactory" traditional practices.

Beginning of Formal Education in Awudome
Formal education and Christianity were introduced into Tsito in the Awudome

Traditional Area in 1886 with the arrival of the Bremen missionaries. The people of Tsito took the challenge of building and attending schools very early and were among the first central Ewe speaking people to build their junior and senior (primary and middle) schools. Pupils were then attracted from the neighbouring towns and villages especially from Abutia, Sokode, Hlefi, Wegbe and from all the other Awudome settlements to attend these schools.

As early as 1949, there was already a nucleus of the educated élite including Messrs. A. K. Asem (the late Principal Secretary of the Ministry of Agriculture), H. K. Addae (the late Magistrate) and the energetic chief of Tsito, the late Togbe Gobo Dake XI of Mark Cofie Engineering fame. The late Togbe saw active service in the 2nd World War in the Far East. Together with those interested in community development and education, they founded the Awudome Educational Bureau to promote education in the area in the late 1940s. They then established the Awudome Institute to train middle school leavers who were adults in the vocations with much emphasis on agriculture. Students of this school were prepared for the London Chamber of Commerce examinations. It was this core of educated men who brought about the idea of the adult college, the focus of this chapter.

In the field of formal education in the Awudome area, Tsito has taken the lead in building schools, and in encouraging attendance. Three second-cycle institutions in the Awudome traditional area, namely Awudome Secondary School, the Awudome Secondary Technical School and Tsito Business College in addition to the Awudome Residential Adult College are all built at Tsito.

The Awudome Residential Community Education Programme

Historical Overview
Already, as has been pointed out, a core of educated individuals had embraced the idea of adult education in the Awudome area. They always organized adult education programmes for community members. Because of their keen interest in adult education, they sent two delegates in the persons of A. K. Asem and H. K. Addae to participate in the first Annual New Year School of the Department of Extra Mural Studies of the University College of the Gold Coast in Komenda in 1949/50.

These two gentlemen were very much enthused by the spirit of voluntarism displayed by participants at Komenda and the commitment to community improvement programmes of the school. (The participants at Komenda enthusiastically constructed wells for the inhabitants). More appealing to them was the high level of free academic discussions and study group work throughout the period of the school.

Messrs. Addae and Asem had an all night meeting with Dr. David Kimble, the then Director of the Department of Extra Mural Studies (DEMS). They wanted a local branch of the People's Educational Association organized in the Awudome area and an Extra-Mural Class at Tsito. They kept their promise with David Kimble and formed the PEA in Awudome with the class centre opened at Tsito, on their return from the school.

In those early years, the Department was well known for its weekend conferences and workshops, one-day schools and public lectures. In the 1950/51 academic year, 24 one-day schools and 15 weekend conferences were organized throughout the country by the Department. The Tsito branch of the PEA hosted one of these programmes. The theme for this workshop was "The Problems of Rural Development in Awudome" (Opare-Abetia, 1980).

At this workshop in January 1950, the Executive of the PEA branch and the youth of Awudome asked for the construction of a residential college at Tsito on the Scandinavian Folk High School model. This was to supplement PEA courses in the community. Dr. Kimble who was at this weekend conference explained that, the Department did not have the resources at its disposal to put up such a centre. He, however, advised participants that, if they could start the construction on their own, the Department would strongly support them.

Immediately after the meeting, clearing started seriously at the site where the College still stands. Twenty-four hours on arrival in Accra, David Kimble received a telegram from Tsito stating, "Site cleared, awaiting pick-axes and shovels" (Opare Abetia, 1980). David Kimble made a frantic effort in launching an appeal to local and international organizations. The appeals he made throughout the world were responded to favourably. People and organizations contributed in cash and kind to make the dream of a residential adult college a reality.

Some of the donor organizations included the PEA, the Voluntary Work Camps Association (VOLU), the Volunteer Service Organization (VSO) from Britain and Danish Women's Association. Others were firms and people in Trans-Volta Togoland (now Volta Region of Ghana) including the Trans-Volta Togoland Council. The rest included the United Nations Educational, Scientific and Cultural Organization (UNESCO) and very many private and governmental organizations. Denmark and North America also generously responded to the appeal and gave both material and financial support. After Lomax Ariba, an architect in Accra, had drawn the site plan and some voluntary contributions had come in, the constructional work began in May 1950. The official foundation stone for the construction of the building was laid on the

December 11, 1950 by David Kimble.

Some of the organizations especially the PEA, the VOLU and the Department of Social Welfare and Community Development took active part in the constructional work of the college. Youth organizations, schools, women groups and divisions of Awudome particularly indigenous organizations and clan divisions in Tsito community, regularly, organized themselves in turn to undertake communal labour to construct the College when financial and material support was received from the donors. Kimble organized some students at the University College, Legon to participate in the constructional work. The enthusiasm and commitment of the people of Awudome in the construction of the collage were highly commendable.

Apart from the communal labour the Awudome community also made a lot of financial and material contributions towards the development of the college. However, "the college, as it is now, is on the whole due to the care, management and material assistance that the Department of Extra-Mural Studies and its successor, the Institute of Adult Education have given over the years" (Opare-Abetia, 1970). The Resident Tutor's bungalow, the multi-purpose hall (used for lectures, dining, entertainment and other social and educational activities) and the bathrooms/toilets are recent extension works undertaken by the Institute.

In all, the college infrastructure consists of twenty-two-bed chalets complete with shower and toilets that can accommodate 40 students. There are four bungalows for administrative staff and course facilitators. A winding access road lined up with avenue trees leads from the Accra-Ho highway to the college, which is romantically built on the crest of a sharp hill overlooking a vast expanse of savanna plains. There are also two halls, which are all purpose, providing space for talks, lecturers, discussions, music and dance.

Mr. and Mrs. Daniel Pederson, sent by the Danish government, participated in building the college. It was with the Pedersons' help that the electricity generator, now abandoned because of the Akosombo hydroelectric power connections, was installed at the college. The generator provided light to promote academic work and social activities at night.

The constructional period of the college fell within the transitional period when the people of the Gold Coast were preparing themselves for political independence. The government then launched a community development scheme in the Gold Coast to bring changes in the outlook of the environment signifying the dawn of a new era. Many communities started to undertake self-help projects and were supported by the government mainly through the Department of Social Welfare and Community Development. The People's Educational Association also initiated and supported some of these projects at

Komenda in the Central Region and Susuanso in the Brong-Ahafo Region. At both places, wells were dug with the support of the PEA and the local people were provided with sources of good drinking water.

At other places, the PEA fostered by the Institute of Adult Education (IAE), undertook community improvement activities like the construction of new latrines, street drains and school buildings. The construction of the college at Tsito, however, was spectacular: it had been built with remarkable speed and completed within a year. The College stands as an everlasting monument to the PEA, the IAE and finally, the people of Awudome after whom the college is named. It remains a unique educational institution in Ghana. It continues to run various types of courses for community members, neighbours and organizations both local and foreign.

The general enthusiasm and speed with which the College was built impressed the last Governor-General of the Gold Coast, the Earl of Listowel and Patron of the College to comment:

> I believe the college is the most interesting and remarkable experiment in education and development that I have seen anywhere in Ghana since my time began (Kimble, 1950).

Original Objectives
The original objectives set for the building of the college included the following:

1. To provide craft courses for both men and women;
2. To serve as a base for other educational activities e.g. literacy;
3. To promote agriculture in the community;
4. To give leadership courses in government to various categories of people including those in voluntary organizations (Opare-Abetia, 1980).

Briefly put, the college was to provide opportunities for education in political, social and vocational fields to help people contribute to the general development process.

To realize some of the objectives stated above, the administrators of the college and members of the Awudome community launched an integrated rural development programme.

The College, the Curriculum and the Community in the Early Years
In the 1973 Silver Jubilee New Year School, the then Chairman of the ruling military regime in Ghana, the National Redemption Council (NRC), noted that:

Theories of Community Education 47

When this University was established twenty-five years ago, it was decided that it should have a Department of Extra-Mural Studies to enable it, among other things, to determine the needs of the community and help in meeting them. But the ordinary person in Ghana today does not see the involvement of our universities in the solution of ordinary problems, largely because the universities are yet to demonstrate to the ordinary person that knowledge can have practical application to the ordinary business of living. (Acheampong speech quoted in Jones Quartey ed., 1974)

General Acheampong's concern was that the Department, for that matter the University of Ghana, was not seen to be playing its role in community development and community education activities. Earlier on in the early 1960s, the late Dr. Kwame Nkrumah the then President of Ghana was more vocal in referring to the Universities as ivory towers which refused to get involved in community development issues. The picture was not all that bleak as expressed by the then army General and President, both deceased.

One might admit that there has been much formalization of the Institute's work and over-concentration on academic courses especially in the Workers' Colleges after 1962. Yet, there are some growth points in community education which give hope for the development of programmes to get communities fully involved in 'University-based" adult education programmes. These help them to improve upon their skills and to solve basic social and economic problems. The Awudome Residential Adult College (ARAC), for example, has, over the years, tried to get people involved in programmes dealing with the fundamental issues affecting their lives. It is a centre for the diffusion of knowledge.

As Kunczik (1985) noted, "a central aspect of any modernization process is the diffusion of innovation". The college's basic objective is to introduce and spread new ideas among its clientele so that they will be able to internalize these ideas to improve upon their skills and environment. The AIDA model (ATTENTION, INTEREST, DESIRE, and ACTION), which has been used in diffusion of innovation, has been adopted by the College's newspaper, the farm and all college programmes in spreading its innovational programmes. The clientele's attention is usually drawn to the innovation in the newspaper and at workshops on the farm and at the College. Clientele's interest is aroused to discuss the issues. As a result, their desire is built through participation and discussion and the net result is that action is usually taken by the clientele to contribute towards the development process.

The basic unit around which the programmes revolve is the adult College. The College runs short residential courses for different categories of people. They include the unemployed youth, local community members, traditional rulers, voluntary organizations and women groups. It has been the responsibility of the College, to arouse their consciousness and organize courses for them. Then, there are categories of people and organizations, which see the need to improve their living standards and that of their workers. These include the Trade Unions, Ghana National Association of Teachers and Ministry of Agriculture.

At this juncture, a close look is taken at the functions of the college and especially at those of its various units, which serve its immediate environs and the larger community. ARAC has always been given a special recognition in local and national development by the Institute of Adult Education. From its early days, the College has, therefore, been mounting both local and national residential courses. This dual character of the college for running courses for both locals and outsiders was emphasized by David Kimble (DEMS Report, 1949/50): The College is to be used not only for the development of the human resource of the community but also of the larger society.

In the 1950s, there were four main types of programmes mounted at the College. These were the evening classes, weekend and vocational courses, and the three months' residential courses. The three-month courses were run at ARAC for about 40 students selected from the evening classes throughout the country. Subjects taught included English Language, Social Studies, West Africa and World History. Piggery was also started (PEA, 1957/58). Some participants and local people were motivated to take to agriculture through these programmes. No effective mechanism was, however, put in place to evaluate the performance of the programme beneficiaries during the 1950s.

The agricultural programme was not remarkably different from the other academic courses run in the formal school system. Agriculture, although an important subject for development and the creation of employment, is essentially a practical subject. It appears that it remained largely an academic subject although no academic certificates were awarded at the end of the programme.

Graduates from the residential courses looked for white-collar jobs. This was the case of graduates from the Folk Development Colleges in Tanzania. It was to make the programme more practical and motivate students to take to agriculture in the field that a Demonstration Farm was established later on as a component of the college programmes.

The government without whose assistance courses would not have taken off the ground sponsored the early courses at the College. In the 1956/57 financial year, for instance, the government gave a grant of £13,000 for the four types of courses mentioned above throughout the country (PEA, 1957/58). The College had its share from this grant to run courses. Courses for

District Commissioners throughout the country were also mounted and sponsored by the central government at the College to enable them to take stock of their performance and formulate strategies for the future. Government sponsorship of these programmes popularized the existence of the College and promoted its sustainability.

In the early years, there were other programmes mounted by the college to improve the living conditions of the local community. A Danish nurse and social worker by name J. Jette Bukke, who was sponsored by Danish Women's Association to the College and the community, lived with the people at Tsito, took part in all social and economic activities and finally wrote a book on the life of the Awudome community.

She worked around the clock on maternal, environmental and child health. It was a one-year health education programme mounted by the Danish nurse. Before then, there were also two-week regular awareness lectures mounted by Miss (now Professor) Lalage Bown, the first resident tutor of the college. She used Tsito as her base, touring different parts of the Volta Region. Her popularity spread all over the Region and she is still recalled and remembered by the popular name Dake Yawa. (Dake is the stool name of the royal house in Tsito and Yawa is a Thursday born female. She was, therefore, made an honorary member of the Tsito royal family).

Quite apart from the national vocational courses launched by the PEA at Tsito, there were other programmes mounted by the college. Firstly, there were evening literacy classes in subjects like Ewe, English and numerals. Secondly, there were workshops for local carpenters and masons. The artisans were engaged in technical drawing and practical work (PEA, 1957/58). Daniel Pedersen a master craftsman, mentioned earlier, was also not only interested in the constructional work of the College. He was also an active adult educator and skills instructor who trained the local people in the crafts. The late Tsiami Kwasi who was a well renowned carpenter, like some other carpenters in the community, learnt or improved upon his carpentry skills from Pedersen's training programmes. It is because of the functional literacy programme mounted by Pederson that there are many competent carpenters in Awudome.

There was the formation of Boys' Club and Women's Associations fostered by the collage to seek the welfare of members and promote the development of the community. Farming experiments with chicken, pigs, sheep and goats, contour ridging, planting of citrus trees and oil palms, coffee and vegetable gardening were made. The courses were popularly patronized but the enthusiasm with which they were started was not sustained over the years. This was because the majority of participants could not market their skills as envisaged. Others could not get either the capital or equipment to start a trade on their own. The situation was further compounded by non-availability of jobs as they graduated from the training provided (PEA, 1957/58).

The initial enthusiasm was, however, highly remarkable. This was within the constructional period, 1950 to 1963. Innovation in adult education experiment kept the people interested in the college activities in those days. It was also due to the commitment of the local community, the goodwill and the collaboration among the various organizations and individuals that the enthusiasm of the people in the project was sustained.

The College, the Community and Social Development Programmes

At independence in 1957 and more particularly after Ghana had attained her republican status in 1960, Ghana needed a new crop of people for her development programmes. More job opportunities were opened in fulfillment of independence promises made by the Convention People's Party (CPP) government. Africanization policy of the public service also began. The orientation of the adult College had to change accordingly. It had to identify new features, which would give a new look to the old ideas during this changing and challenging period.

In full recognition of the fact that the College was to respond to local and national needs, an enthusiastic attempt was made to promote adult education opportunities for the majority in and out the community. A brief discussion of some educational and social programmes organized by the College as a centre for development to respond to some of these needs is presented below.

The College and the Community
One of the features of Folk High Schools is to make its facilities available for community use and also engage school staff in community education and development programmes. Thus, the adult College compound is open to the citizens for use as a centre for educational programmes and meetings. The college staff members are also involved in community activities of various orientations. Many of the important meetings and workshops organized by the various local organizations and especially the residential programmes are held at the College at low cost to either the community organizers or participants.

The people of Awudome receive their important visitors at the College. The visit of two high-ranking women, the former Canadian High Commissioner to Ghana, Miss Sandelle Scrimshaw, and the then Director of the Institute of Adult Education, Professor Miranda Greenstreet to Tsito was quite significant for the community as a whole in 1988. Their visit provided an opportunity for Tsito chiefs and elders to re-assess the role of their own women. A folk-singing group composed entirely of women, gorgeously dressed with voices far-reaching was singing as it moved along to the College:

> The prejudice of man
> Has shifted the role of women to the background.
> Can men do it without women?
> Can women do it without men?

The chief of Tsito, Togbe Gobo Dake, in his welcome speech let his eyes run all around the circle of young and old in a dignified manner. Then, he suggested: "Let the presence of these two ladies, the one from here and the other from the far place across the sea among us today, inspire you, our mothers and daughters, to follow the examples of those, who through hard work, have reached the top of their professions. One way to achieve such heights is to plan your lives, set visions and aspire to realize your visions". The Queenmother who replied on behalf of the women folk accepted the challenge.

Since then, women groups have intensified their female education campaigns. The compound is very alive during local festive days such as during yam festivals and Easter celebrations. On these occasions, the College is fully utilized by citizens. The "Town Hall", which is the biggest hall on the College premises, is regularly used as the most convenient place where the community holds its dances and social functions. One would not be surprised to witness three consecutive days of entertainment in the hall during festival periods or during the Yuletide. Course participants also take part in these social activities with the local people.

When courses are in progress, course participants usually, from outside the community, pay homage to the local chief and elders. The chief and other local dignitaries and citizens are invited to chair opening and closing ceremonies or deliver a speech. The various local cultural drumming groups are also invited to entertain course participants. Participants are encouraged to go on visit to town, live with the people and share their joys and sorrows. Arrangements are made for participants to attend church services in town, and participate in ceremonies and festivals.

Hardly can anyone differentiate between course participants and citizens at these functions, as they all participate together. The effects of community and college participation in common programmes may be great. The results may not be immediate. Much cross-fertilization of ideas takes place since courses are very regular at the College and there is close relationship between course participants and the local people.

Attempts have been made to bring the University of Ghana, Legon, to the people of Awudome. By this, lecturers and Directors of the Institute of Adult Education from Legon pay working visits to the people and the College. Among these were Dr. G. K. Bluwey, then a lecturer of the Political Science Department of the University of Ghana. Dr. Bluwey started a series of lectures on political issues in 1980 in the "Afegame" (the original stool house of Tsito). He spoke about *Principles of Government, the Rights and Responsibilities of the Government, The Rights and Responsibilities of Local Rulers and Citizens.* It was a popular series involving the elders and Tsito citizens as a whole.

Other lecture topics delivered by experts at Tsito included *the Police as a Friend and Multi-Party Constitutional Rule in Ghana.* Mr. T. K. Adzoe (1991) of the National Commission for Democracy declared at one of the lectures, "... despite morbid fears and misgivings against political parties, if parties were operated by honest and dedicated citizens, they would be seen as invaluable tools in the practice of democracy. They would ensure that laws which are inimical to the people are not made".

The Institute of Adult Education organizes educational programmes with foreign visitors also to share educational and development ideas with the local community. Thus, there were lecturers invited from Universities or renowned educational organizations the world over to Tsito. They included Professor Paul Fordham, the Dean of the Faculty of Educational Studies and Director of the Department of Adult Education of the University Southampton, Mr. K. Grytli of Norway, Mr. Paul Hearse from Britain, both from their respective adult education institutions. Others included Mr. Paul Bertelsen a Dane and former Chief of Adult Education, UNESCO and Miss Eva Rude of the Danish Women Association. Eva Rude helped the people of Tsito to put up a kindergarten.

At durbars, visitors promised to give support in recognition of the people's efforts towards development programmes. Some of these promises were honoured. Newsprints for *Kpodoga* publication were provided as Grytli promised. Literacy classes were opened and literacy materials were provided to the community as Paul Bertelsen promised.

There were also organizations like the Danish Women Association and the German Adult Education Association, which organized workshops and durbars with the people through the College. These contacts have as much educational value for the local people as they have for the visitors and sponsoring organizations. It could be said that the impact of all the collaborative activities discussed above influenced the course of development in Tsito. Thus, Tsito took the lead in community development work among the Awudome towns. It, for instance, built a health post, two secondary schools and a vocational/secretarial school, all to serve the Awudome community. Among the Awudome community, Tsito was the first to be provided with pipe borne water and electric power hooked to the Akosombo grid.

Quite apart from the occasional lectures and visits from people outside, other educational programmes have been organized in collaboration with various local groups. In the 1970s, the college with local PEA members built a chop bar (a rural restaurant). The purpose was to expose chop bar keepers in the area to modern methods of running and maintaining chop bars. The bar served as a centre for lessons on nutrition and home management to the girls and women in the area. It provided a decent eating-place to the locals as well as visitors.

The main objective of these programmes is to help the rural community members feel that they are a part of the larger community and prepare them know that they have a say and a part to play in the government of their community. They must also be linked to people outside their communities.

The Mathew's Choir

The Danish Folk High Schools are noted for the tradition in music development and community singing. Great names, as discussed earlier on, were associated with this tradition. Adult College also attempts to adopt this tradition. In view of this, the College has adopted Mathew's Choir, a cultural and choral group, formed in the early 1970s, by a group of Tsito citizens. The big name associated with this music tradition is Mathew Adzaku, after whom the choir is named. With the adoption of this group by ARAC in the early 1980s, the choir has diversified its functions. Awudome Residential Adult College has planned a series of educational programmes with members of the choir.

A literacy class has been established for the choir members who could not write or read. Within a period of six months, all the members could read the words of the songs they learnt. Another important component of the literacy programme is music appreciation. All learn to identify the keys and read them so that they can learn songs faster and appreciate how songs are composed. They have greatly improved their performances as a result of learning music appreciation. They usually receive invitations to entertain participants with their songs at conferences at the college and at New Year Schools of the Institute of Adult Education. They attend funerals and festivals to mourn the dead and entertain guests at functions organized by their members, the community or outsiders as appropriate.

Members also learn basic accounting principles. With basic and domestic accounting, traders and housewives in the choir learn how to reckon their income and expenditure daily or within a specified period. They learn capital, income and expenditure, profit and loss theories and practices. Not all, we may concede, understand the lessons. But some impact is made. The majority of them claim that they make conscious efforts to record their income and expenditure in their businesses. They have been advised to record whatever amount they invest in any business, project or family affairs and reckon the profits and losses involved. This good attempt to introduce the local community to basic principle of accounts is very popularly and well patronized by members. Occasionally, the group undertakes environmental cleaning activities. They clean the two markets in the town regularly. They have constructed incinerators at the outskirts of the town for the disposal of refuse by the community.

The Mathew's Choir took a step further ahead of other groups in Tsito to learn some skills and handicrafts. Fishing is popular in river Tsawe, which flows through Anyirawase, Tsawenu and Tsito lands. The male members, therefore, learn to weave fishing nets for fishing. These nets are used by members of the choir and by men of these towns for fishing. Fishing expeditions have, therefore, become popular among the people of Awudome. Women in the area have become fishmongers. Fishing and fish marketing have become lucrative jobs for the people. These broaden the economic base of the people and improve their living standards and protein intake. The female members of the Choir also learn embroidery, buttonholing, stitching, handkerchief and tablecloth making. They learn about home management. All these programmes mentioned above are undertaken in collaboration with ARAC who usually organizes facilitators for them.

Mr. R. J. Mettle Nunoo, then co-ordinator of Non-Formal Education Division of the Ministry of Education visited the group in 1987. He noted with satisfaction that if their efforts in functional literacy learning were replicated in many towns, there would be a great leap in the whole country's development process.

Residential Courses for Citizens and Residents
Like the Folk High Schools, the Awudome programme continues to organize courses at the college for community members to respond to demands of the times. With the change in the College orientation in the early 1960s, as mentioned earlier, the longer vocational and professional courses were rather discontinued. Only short residential courses continue to be run. A number of these courses are organized for the local residents in the Awudome traditional

area. Some of these courses are organized for those in leadership positions in different organizations and groups in the area. Among such courses run in recent years for Awudome communities were those for the executive members of Area, Zonal and Unit Committees, voluntary groups, clan leaders, chiefs, elders and queenmothers, women, religious and occupational groups like the seamstresses, carpenters and tailors.

During the courses, participants go through the history of Awudome. The need for unity among the people and collaboration among the various institutions in the area are also emphasized for purposes of social cohesion and community development. The rights and responsibilities of various leaders and those of their groups are extensively discussed.

For the chief and elders, emphasis at the workshops centres on the modernization and preservation of the institution of chieftaincy, the role of elders in the maintenance of discipline in the community and the need for a united front among elders. They also discuss cultural activities and try to modernize obsolete customs like widowhood rites. Elders set a code of behaviour for themselves to live exemplary lives. An action programme for the development of Awudome has been drawn at the end of each of these workshops.

The College mounts leadership and human relations workshops specifically for the female teachers of educational institutions in Awudome. Here again, the important role played in society by women has been taken into consideration. It is also to reinforce their role as community builders and first line teachers in the home and the community.

Leadership and management workshops have been organized for all heads of educational institutions in the community. These workshops for the heads of the educational institutions are very important. When dynamic and enlightened heads of schools pursue sound administrative procedures, the schools will achieve much for the community. The heads learnt to work together, practised shared leadership with their counterpart teachers and promoted the formation of parent-teacher associations. These associations, bridging the gap between the community and the school administration, maintain discipline and raise academic standards. Since then, parent-teacher associations in the area have been functioning quite successfully. As a result also, school heads have been working closely with the chief and the council of elders, youth organizations, and the churches.

Other workshops for the residents included those for middle school, junior and senior secondary school leavers and the unemployed youth on possibilities for self-employment. As a result, some joined apprenticeships in tailoring and carpentry. Others have started as farmers. All the courses mentioned above were popularly patronized. Courses were organized for traditional birth attendants to upgrade their occupational competence and enhance personal and environmental hygiene.

Quite apart from these workshops and programmes organized specifically for the local people, residents are always invited to participate in other programmes organized by the Institute. These workshops usually end up with local plans for the future development of their respective areas of operation. The courses and programmes organized for the local people are all meant to arouse their consciousness to enhance their personal and community development. The various groups including women, the youth, the chief and elders and teachers all meet to assess their work and plan for the future. At all the courses, participants are advised on how to form groups so that with a common front they can develop together and support community and national development efforts.

Participants at these community workshops sing local and national songs designed to encourage hard work, patriotism and good moral living as is done in the Folk High Schools. The College, as an educational powerhouse, is thus used for mobilization towards development in Awudome. The College tries to meet the community half way by organizing workshops for some groups. The College moves down to the majority at the local level. There is a need for staff to know their problems and aspirations; and this is done through the participation in festivals, bargaining with them at the market place, sharing jokes at leisure, working with them and supporting their development programmes.

Apart from workshops for and working with the various local groups mentioned above, the staff of the College promote other different types of social and health education activities. Some of these are briefly discussed below.

Sporting and Cultural Activities
One influence of the integrated rural development programme is the tendency of the local community members to belong to bodies such as cultural groups, co-operatives and sporting clubs. The main objective is to use sporting, cultural and other social activities to promote the physical, mental, and spiritual growth of the youth and to encourage social interaction in order to strengthen the community towards development. On a less serious note, it is to get them involved in the project activities so that the community newspaper, *Kpodoga*, could cover them. In May 1995, therefore, the Tsito Sports and Cultural Association (TSCA) was formed. This Association is affiliated to the International Sports and Culture Association with headquarters in Denmark

(ISCA, 1995). Consequently, the first two ISCA meetings held in Africa were held at Awudome Residential Adult College, Tsito in February 1998 and in January 1999 respectively. Representatives from five countries namely Ghana, Mauritius, South Africa, Uganda and Denmark with special representatives from TSCA, DGI and UNESCO participated in the conference. Outlined Policies of Sports in Africa were presented and discussed by conference participants (ARAC Report, 1999). A welcome outcome of the second ISCA conference is the interest expressed by the UNESCO representative to develop the facilities of ARAC to an appreciable level to be used not only for ISCA meetings but also for other international training programmes.

So far, two members of TSCA have taken part in four-month leadership training and sporting and cultural courses in Folk High Schools in Denmark. Three youths from TSCA also had a three-week familiarization tour of Folk High Schools in 1996. In 1997, TSCA took part in a seminar on "Sports For All" in Zimbabwe while in 1998 representatives from DGI came to ARAC to train the youth in sporting activities. In the same year, members of the TSCA took part in volleyball tournament and cultural troupe performance in Denmark.

As a result of the participation of the youth in these programmes, there is a new wave of sporting and cultural activities in the Awudome community. TSCA has become a member of the Ghana Football Association Second Division Football League in the Volta Region. The Tsito Cultural Troupe has also improved upon its performance and is frequently featured on the Volta Star FM Radio at Ho. Their performances at ARAC and at functions have become very impressive and highly educative.

The Awudome Health Centre
A necessary component of an integrated rural development project like the Awudome project is the development of the health sector of the people. As mentioned earlier on, two Danish health and social workers, with ARAC as their base of operation, worked among the Awudome community to help them improve their health and social life. But these were not enough to satisfy the health needs of the local community. The Danish International Development Agency (DANIDA) was contacted by the women of Tsito to help in the construction of a health centre because of her long established relationship that developed between the College and the Awudome community.

DANIDA willingly obliged and released an amount of ¢127,329,596.53 through the Danish Embassy in Ghana, for the construction of a health centre and a KVIP (Welcome Address of Tsito Women's Association on the Occasion of the Commissioning of the Tsito Health Centre, 1998). According to this address, the clinic and the KVIP, which were started on December 10, 1992 near ARAC, were handed over to the Awudome community in 1995.

The scope of the Awudome community education development project was thus expanded. The health centre has become an institution for public health education and medical care for the people of the Awudome Traditional Area. Family life, personal hygiene and environmental education programmes are launched to help improve the health needs of the people.

General Course Offerings at the Awudome Residential Adult College

As mentioned earlier on, the College offers its facilities to other organizations to run programmes. One such important series of programmes run at the College is on Indigenous Cultural Beliefs and Practices and the Catholic Christian Faith. The aims of the series organized by a commission appointed by the Keta-Ho Diocese of the Catholic Church are:

1. To make the Catholic more and more confident in his/her attitude towards the indigenous beliefs and customs of our people;

2. To help the Ghanaian of Keta-Ho Diocese to understand deeper the culture into which he/she has been born so that he/she can help preserve the richness of our culture for national development (Catholic Secretariat, 1988).

The essence of the programme was to integrate local values into the Christian religion. Issues discussed in the series were customary functions of the chief or the queen, installation and stool cleansing. The commission did not see much wrong with these practices for Christian chiefs. However, it felt that some dehumanizing ceremonies connected with installation, confinement and polygamous marriage must be discouraged. Burial ceremonies of victims of tragic deaths were discussed. The commission did not see the reason why special ceremonies should be organized for such burials. It was recommended that these practices must be stopped because they are against the country's laws. Other issues discussed were witchcraft, herbal treatment, ancestral worship, taboos, traditional songs and the worship of objects. The discussions of the commission were in response to a chain of reactions from some Ghanaians who felt that they were losing their traditional values, their literature, songs, tales, praise chants, drum beats, and the beauty and wisdom of the sayings of the elders.

The Catholic programme acknowledged the presence of traditional beliefs in the community and suggested that some of these beliefs must be accepted but in a modernized and refined form.

Development Education and Leadership Services (DELES) Workshops
David Kimble saw the importance of the College for the whole nation and for the world at large as discussed earlier on. It was for this reasons that he advised that the facilities of the College should be made available for others outside the community. Different types of courses for various national and international professional groups are either hosted or organized by the College. These courses have made the college popular nationally and internationally.

One of the regular and popular leadership programmes organized by the College is the Development Education and Leadership Services (DELES). It is a new approach in leadership training programmes. Although, the DELES programme has its philosophy and principles guiding it, it has not got a fixed syllabus for its clientele. Participants determine the content of their own programme. On the day of arrival, participants explain the problems they meet with and the successes they make at their workplaces and communities. They explain the nature of their work in details.

They go on to state the types of skills they would like to acquire or what they expect to learn from the workshop to build and improve their leadership skills. Some common expectations include: how to communicate better with colleagues; how to motivate subordinates; how to live with other people; how to solve problems; how to mobilize people for action; how to build and sustain people's interest and how to become a good leader. Through the use of codes in the form of role-plays, skits, group work, reflection followed by discussions relating to real life situations, participants see their problems mirrored to them.

Through discussions, they arrive at suggested solutions to the problems that they may adopt on their return to their workplaces. The programme is based on Christian and traditional communal spirit of brotherhood. Respect for the dignity of the lowly placed in society and workplace is emphasized. The leadership-training programme starts with the concrete experience of all participants. It continues with everybody teaching and everybody learning. It is a programme characterized by continuous reflection and action resulting in the transformation of participants, their environment and the society as a whole. It is to break the "culture of silence" into which many workers and people are placed (Freire, 1974).

Thus, the DELES programme has laid emphasis on the constant and regular meeting with the facilitators and the participants to refresh their memories. It is not once-for-all experience. It promotes a constant renewal of effort, insight, questioning and understanding. In brief, the process is on going. Participants hold regular formal meetings at four-month intervals. Leaders from organizations are always registered for this programme so as to produce an everlasting stream of leaders for organizations. The first and second groups of participants registered local people such as Togbe Buatsi, a sub-chief and member of council of elders, Mr. Kofi Dose the secretary of the Mathew's Choir and Miss Akorfa Kettey, the secretary of Awudome Women Farmers' League, and a number of citizens from the area.

Since the programme started in February 1986, a large number of mid-level supervisors, administrators, and people in leadership positions in very many organizations throughout the country have participated in the DELES workshops at Tsito. Some of these organizations are the National Mobilization Programme, the Adventist Development and Relief Agency, Akosombo Textiles Ltd. and Juapong Textiles Ltd. Others include the Ghana Textiles Printing Company, the Volta River Authority, the 31st December Women's Movement, Ministry of Health, the various member-unions of the Trade Union Congress, the Ghana Education Service, and many Dioceses of the Catholic Church. Individuals and voluntary organizations have all participated in the workshops. The College serves as a base for the spread of DELES throughout the country. The ripple effects have been felt and organizations invite facilitators from the College to organize DELES workshops for them throughout the country.

Certificate Course in Adult Education
Several attempts have also been made to start formal education programme at the College on permanent basis. One of the latest attempts in this direction is the introduction of a certificate course in adult education at the College. This programme is to train adult educators for various organizations for grassroots community and adult education work in the country. This is considered important because many people who work as adult educators, extension officers and trainer of trainers in many organizations do not receive any training in the field of adult education. It was with this view that attempts have been made to mount adult education programmes for the various organizations, which use adult educators in the promotion of their work.

After all the negotiations had been fully exhausted by the Institute of Adult Education, the Faculty of Social Studies and the Academic Board of the University of Ghana, the Registrar of the University wrote finally on July 31, 1992 to the Director of the Institute of Adult Education granting the latter permission to start the certificate course in Adult Education at the Awudome Residential Adult College, Tsito.

The programme took off as scheduled. In September, 1992 the first batch of 20 students was registered. The yearly intake of students is twenty, according to the University quota system for the Institute of Adult Education. The academic staff of the Institute from its centres at Ho, Tsito, Koforidua and Accra continues to teach the course at the College.

In the 1997/98 academic year when the intake was 21, 19 of the students were teachers drawn from the Ghana Education Service (GES) and only two were non-teachers. One of the two was from the education department of the Ghana Monuments and Museums Board while the other was a chief from Buipe in the Northern Region of Ghana.

When asked in a newspaper interview (*Kpodoga*, October 1997) how his interest in the certificate course started, the chief responded:

> Someone introduced Adult Education to me as a programme very suitable for a community leader or a chief. Part of the interview by *Kpodoga* Editor with the chief translated from *Kpodoga* No. 64 October 1997 is reproduced below.

Northern Chief Back to School:

Question: Welcome Na. Can we start by telling us what brought you down south to Tsito?

Answer: I am at Tsito studying for the University of Ghana's Certificate Course in Adult Education for one year.

Question: You have moved and taken residence far away from your subjects. How do they take to that?

Answer: Some of my people felt bad about my absence. But now they are all happy to have an educated chief and congratulated me for my admission into the University.

Question: How do you find the course?

Answer: The course is very suitable for a community leader or a chief as it covers areas like Community Education and Mobilization, Adult Teaching Methods, Literacy Education, Leadership Skills, Counselling, Programme Planning and Management and Adult Psychology. I have gained the impression that this course can bring up leaders in whatever capacity they may serve.

Question: Do you have opportunities to interact with the community outside the university campus?

Answer: My fellow students and I have made a courtesy call on the chief of Tsito and his elders. I have also reached some houses and family levels and interacted with individuals. I also attend the Methodist Church in town. I am impressed by the spirit of self-help in Tsito.

The people have achieved a lot without putting their hopes on government to do things for them. I have learnt a lot both in the classroom and in the community to enhance my work among my people after my course.

The participation of traditional rulers and all categories of leaders in this certificate programme is very important as Buipe Na A. R. Adam stated. It helps in the mobilization of people in the process of community development.

Some Other Courses

Apart from the course organized by the Catholic Church briefly discussed above, there are several programmes organized by other organizations. These include courses organized by the British Council for the Consultants of the Management Development and Productivity Institute; the Netherlands sponsored course for para-medical staff of Ministry of Health; the study tour by the German Adult Education Association; and workshop for Catholic Women's Association. Other courses were for the Managers of the Social Security and National Insurance Trust, officials of the Primary Health Care Unit of the Ministry of Health, the Regional Registrars of the National House of Chiefs, the various Unions of the Ghana Trade Union Congress and the Water and Sanitation Project. The DANIDA-sponsored water utilization projects were the most regular at the college in 1998 and 1999.

The Ghana Army finds ARAC a convenient place to camp soldiers for military exercises in the surrounding forest and rocky hillside. The students of the Geology Department of the University of Ghana use the College yearly as a base to do field work and study the rock formation of the Ewe Ranges on which the College is built.

The Institute of Adult Education collaborates with some organizations to organize workshops and other organizations concerned. This was in the case of the study tour and workshop for the German Adult Education Association. An extensive three-week tour of Ghana by 15 German Adult Education officials took the Germans to low-income groups, farm fields, handicraft centres and village artisans. This study tour was rounded off with a forum held at the College. Here the Germans put a number of questions to a team of officials from the Institute of Adult Education, Ministry of Agriculture, the Department of Community Development and the National Council on Women and Development to clarify their experience in the field.

Some of the questions sought to find out why there are many broken-down agricultural machines; what attempts were made to revive the cocoa industry; whether traditional belief has anything to do with immunization and why there were more women than men working on the fields (*African Review,* 1988).

Another important programme jointly organized was that with the Ho District Assembly. It is common knowledge that every local government as well as central government requires money to finance her expenditure. Most of these must come from taxes. Yet, there has been lower-than-expected revenue coming to the District Assembly coffers. To remedy the situation, the Institute of Adult Education accepted invitations from the Ho District Assembly to share ideas on effective revenue collection with the district revenue collectors. This was in 1998.

After sharing experiences on their performance, their successes and problems, the 30 revenue collectors were taken through an exercise of self-criticism which included a reflection of their unpleasant manner of speaking to tax payers and their inability to account for moneys collected. Participants realized that some of the problems of embezzlement and inaccurate accounting processes arose from poverty, illiteracy and ignorance as well as downright disobedience on the part of tax collectors. The workshop then, had the responsibility of leading participants to discover techniques that could be used to fight the various problems. They learnt to talk in a friendlier manner with the taxpayers, relate more cordially with them and account for moneys collected promptly.

At the end of the one week workshop, the Ho District Chief Executive noted happily that they were able to "identify constraints in revenue mobilization and would definitely improve revenue generation in the district."Feedback from the District Chief Executive revealed that collection targets doubled in subsequent months.

Kpodoga, The Rural Community Newspaper

Introduction
In a country such as Ghana where the rural dwellers constitute the larger percentage of the population (70 per cent), all development efforts that expect to meet with a reasonable amount of success must take into account the conditions of the rural people. Until recently, this had not been the case. Little consideration had been given to the rural areas in development planning. This has had adverse effects on the development of the nation as a whole. In order to quicken the development process of the rural areas, planners are now forging

out specially-designed programmes and projects for the rural sector. These include the production of rural newspapers to bridge the communication gap between the rural and urban areas. Communities need to be sensitized to participate in the development process.

Ghana is predominantly an agricultural country whose inhabitants require information on all types of subjects relating to soil conservation, nutrition, the running of small co-operatives and many more. While a newspaper message can reach thousands of people simultaneously, a large number of extension officers might spend much time carrying the same message to an equivalent number of people. Faced with the perennial problem of rural-urban migration, Ghana is in need of newspapers that can draw the attention of disenchanted youth to the best that they can make out of the land.

Thousands of children drop out of the elementary schools each year while thousands more adults graduate from the literacy circles. All these people are in danger of relapsing into illiteracy for lack of reading materials. Even if the national newspapers reach the villages, they do so at irregular times. Set up at the urban centres in Accra and Kumasi and published in a foreign language, that is English, the national newspapers seem to be catering for the higher level of the literate class. A rural newspaper, therefore, offers the potential for reducing the isolation of the rural dwellers from their urban counterparts. It is not produced to compete with the national newspapers but used in conjunction with them to supplement the efforts of one another and contribute to overall national development. Specifically, the rural newspaper is produced to promote literacy and rural development.

On the attainment of political independence, the various African states began to appreciate the need for rapid increase in education and economic development. They also believed in the ability of the mass media to communicate messages among all those involved in development. So apart from the existing foreign language daily newspapers, the African governments introduced monthly publications in their major local languages. Examples came from Tanzania, Kenya, Ghana, Nigeria, Gabon, Mali, Senegal, Benin and Togo. The Ghana government produced monthly publications in the major Ghanaian languages for nearly three decades beginning from the 1950s. Some of the newspapers were the *Nkwantabisa* (in Twi), the *Matabiala* (in Ewe) and the *Mansralo* (in Ga).

A few years after the government local language newspapers ceased publication, two departments of the University of Ghana, namely, the School of Communication Studies in 1975 and the Institute of Adult Education in 1976 started publishing similar newspapers for the benefit of rural dwellers. The focus of this paper is, however, on *Kpodoga*.

The History of Kpodoga

The Awudome Residential Adult College publishes the rural newspaper *Kpodoga* meaning a gong-gong, an instrument that symbolizes information or news in the community. Before the publication of the paper, participatory research was conducted in the prospective circulation zone. This was intended to find out the literacy level of the target reading population, their inclination to read, their interests and concerns. This participatory research was necessary for community members to accept the newspaper as their own right from the start and, therefore, contribute to its success.

It was evident from the research that agriculture was the main concern of the target population. It was, however, felt that a rural programme should help improve every aspect of the daily lives of the people in covering their cultural, economic and political activities. It should be as varied as possible so that it can attract a wide readership.

Kpodoga has thus been established for these reasons:

1. To provide the people an opportunity to read about news which they themselves make;

2. To equip readers with skills which will make their lives meaningful;

3. To provide interesting reading material for new literates who can easily relapse into illiteracy if they do not get such reading materials (First Anniversary Report of the Rural Community Paper, Kpodoga, 1977).

Kpodoga was started with UNESCO assistance in April 1976. For the first five years of its operation (1976–1981), it was sponsored by this UN agency. In its initial stages, it was printed by the Information Services Department, Accra. The issues delayed unnecessarily because the Information Services suspended publication in favour of government materials. The initial circulation of the paper was 2,500. It rose to 5,000 in 1977 and 6,000 in 1981. (Fordham, 1982). Publication then slowed down in 1982 because of lack of newsprint.

The second phase of *Kpodoga* dates from October 1987 when earlier in the year Mr. Kare Grytli, a Norwegian adult educator, paid a visit to Tsito. The opportunity was utilized by the project staff and Awudome community to request for newsprint to resume *Kpodoga* publications. In August 1987, the Institute received a large consignment of newsprint from Norway. After several years of dormancy, the rural newspaper *Kpodoga* reappeared on the newsstands in October 1987. The Institute of Adult Education had then taken over the printing aspect of the paper, from the Information Services Department. Since then, the print run has been 2,000 copies per issue.

Organization, Administration and Target Groups of Kpodoga

Over the years, the four-page newspaper concentrated on the coverage of events in the Ho district alone. Tsito was chosen as the rural newspaper's editorial centre because the Institute already had a residential College at Tsito as a component of the integrated rural project. Lack of printing facilities at Tsito, however, makes it necessary for the actual printing of the newspaper to be done outside its environment.

Since it is important that the community must accept the people who publish a rural newspaper, *Kpodoga* has its staff recruited from and resident within the newspaper's coverage area. This brings the staff of the paper into close contact with their target readers and makes them alive to rural problems. This arrangement gives the opportunity to staff to report these problems, as they exist. The staff of the newspaper and elected members of the community constitute the editorial board. This board elects its own chairperson and recruits stringers who are trained in news reporting. It also encourages regular news collection, editing and circulation. The board advises reporters to provide news items, which reflect local conditions and activities. The rural newspaper is thus perceived as preoccupied with the details of activities, values and aspirations present in a given rural community.

The early community newspapers were doing well in interpreting government policies to the people. But by definition, the community newspaper must show the village to the villagers. What they were found more to be doing was to represent the rural environment by political speeches, official handouts and reports on visits to the villages by government officials. In addition, they translated relevant stories from the national newspapers into the local languages.

The Impact of The Rural Newspaper Kpodoga

In the first anniversary ceremony of *Kpodoga* at Anyirawase in 1977, Professor Kwasi Ampene, the then Director of the Institute, noted that the objectives of the paper as discussed above, had been realized and much more has been achieved than expected. The newspaper provides a vehicle for the people to create and write their own news. Many of the articles in the paper are news items and feature articles written by the people themselves. The full-time member of staff on *Kpodoga* publications, the editor, only edits these items and provides the editorials.

An important feature of *Kpodoga* is the representation of local situations — projects and programmes, failures and successes back to the people. As the local people see their pictures and achievements in the local paper, they become excited and motivated to achieve more. They accept the challenge to correct their mistakes. This makes it an immediately useful tool for building self-confidence.

An equally important feature of *Kpodoga* is that it gives publicity to local events and organizations. As these news items are given coverage, they are spread to wide areas for people to learn from them. Without this publicity given to local events, there may be only rumors, gossips and tales in the community.

Dr. Frank C. Laubach, a foremost exponent of adult literacy, for instance, has been worried about follow-up literacy materials for new and even old literates. *Kpodoga* in this sense has a very useful role to play in providing reading materials for both groups. Those who relapse into illiteracy because they cannot get materials to read, revive their reading habits by reading *Kpodoga*. Seeing and reading their own news give the local people psychological satisfaction and serve as a morale booster in arousing their interest in reading.

The favourable literacy environment is now reinforced by the use of *Kpodoga* and the fear of relapsing into illiteracy is minimized. The community newspaper *Kpodoga* or the Announcer has also popularized the writing and reading of the local language, Ewe. It encourages people to treasure their mother tongue, and to continue to write, read and speak it.

The use of mother tongue in community newspaper production and literacy work is very important. Local people know the names of items, pronunciation of words, proverbs and sentence construction and idioms. What they lack are skills for reading and writing. By the use of local language, participants hold discussions in readers clubs intelligently, tell stories excitingly, give examples accurately and read with understanding. All actively participate in discussions.

As a result, participants are excited about their successful active participation in the dialogical pedagogues. They become anxious to learn to improve upon skills learnt and contribute towards community development. The production of newspapers in the mother tongue, therefore, enhances active participation of people in the learning and the development process, as examples of Readers Clubs will illustrate.

A columnist, Stephen Amekli, regularly writes on some common grammatical errors and popular expressions in Ewe so as to keep people's interest in learning new things and revising the old. Amekli was a member of the two-nation (Ghana-Togo) committee, which revised Ewe grammar developed by the Germans in the 19th century. He uses his expertise as a member of the committee not only to up-date the standard of Ewe in his column, but also to discuss the various aspects of the grammar revised by the committee. Readers of Ewe, therefore, update their knowledge on the modern standard Ewe grammar jointly revised by the two Ewe speaking countries.

Kpodoga tries to promote culture by giving a wide coverage to festivals and customary practices in the circulation zone of the paper since 1987. Yam festival, conspicuously the most popular festival among the Ewes, has been widely covered each year signifying the importance of the festival. Yam festivals in Tsito, Have and Sokode have featured in *Kpodoga*, with all the games, customs and lessons connected with them. Yam festivals of other towns in the circulation zone are also publicized because of their educational value. One main lesson from the festivals is that people must learn to work hard and cultivate yams. They learn to work together and celebrate together.

The installation and outdooring of chiefs and queenmothers in Nkwanta and Tsito both in the Awudome Traditional Area featured in the paper. The paper has highlighted the lessons emerging from these ceremonies and institutions. Communities must use festivals as occasions for stocktaking of their development projects and planning for the future. Readers must know what each festival stands for. They identify themselves as members of one community during the celebrations. The paper also discusses what they must not do or what they must do to contribute to the development process.

The last issue of 1997, *Kpodoga* No. 64, threw light on what the local people were doing. There were four news items on the front page of this edition. The lead story carried the story: Botoku Elects Community Development Officers at a General Meeting. The officers were Delali Woadekpor (Health), Janet Gbadagba (Water), Kwami Kuti (Education), Nelson Ampoti (Community Cleanliness), Kodzo Menayor (Roads). Botoku citizens resident outside the community were invited to take part in this important meeting which was addressed by Togbe Tamtia V. Togbe advised all to contribute effectively towards the development of the town.

The second news item was titled "Chief Swears Town's Oath on Wee-Smokers". The chief of Gbefi summoned all citizens to a community meeting and swore the town's oath declaring wee cultivation, marketing and smoking illegal in the town. Any citizen caught taking part in any of these activities was to purify the gods of the town with a ram, two bottles of schnapps, one pot of palm wine and an amount of ¢50,000 cash. It became very necessary to swear this oath because the entire township was engulfed in sadness when the news broke out that an elder with other citizens were imprisoned ten years each for the cultivation of the herb.

The third item, Charcoal Burners Destroy Forest, was the theme of a lecture delivered by Togbe Gbogbo V, the paramount chief of Adaklu Traditional Area at his outdooring ceremony. He warned the people against bush and charcoal burning and advised them to undertake agroforestry practices.

The fourth item discouraged cigarette smoking among drumming groups. Sebastian Dzamposu the leader of Agbeyeye Drumming Group of Tsito outlined the disadvantages of cigarette smoking. Briefly put, cigarette smoking is injurious to the health of the smoker and people close to him. Dzamposu advised entertainment groups and associations against accepting and smoking cigarettes and drinking alcohol.

The only picture at the front page of the paper showed three women trained as community health workers by the Institute of Adult Education at Ho. They were among 30 village social and health workers drawn from different parts of the Volta Region for a community health education workshop. They returned to their communities to educate people on good personal and environmental hygiene practices.

All the news items at the front page of the newspaper, like those at the other pages dealt with personal and community development issues. They did not concentrate on the same personalities but covered a wide range of issues in many communities.

People read the paper for leisure and for other reasons. At a more serious level, it generates a lot of discussion particularly, when readers come together. People would like to discuss the issues with many other people and even if possible take action to improve the community together.

The possibility that readers might have been aware of the need to form readers' clubs cannot be discounted. However, they tended to lack the requisite leadership skills to start the clubs. The College, in collaboration with existing community leadership structures, has provided the stimulus for the fostering of new groups, *Kpodoga* Readers' Clubs.

Kpodoga Readers' Clubs

Readers of *Kpodoga*, at the various centres, come together to form Readers' Clubs. These clubs are scattered over the 60 circulation centres in the Volta Region. However, the majority can be found in the Awudome Traditional Area and in the immediate communities surrounding Awudome. New ones are springing up and some slumbering ones are resuscitating. Their survival and vibrancy depend on the regularity of the paper but time and again the publication of the paper delays. This is blamed on technical difficulties faced by the printers at Legon.

There are many reasons why emphasis is laid on the formation of these clubs. Among others, some of the intentions are to use the clubs to provide face-to-face contact for learners and newspaper staff, to improve feedback and to help members learn how to read and write. Other reasons why the functioning of the clubs are important include the need to enable readers to know one another's problems and achievements and also to help the less educated to understand the content of the newspaper.

Membership of the clubs is open to both literate and illiterate adults of the community. The papers are read aloud and all discuss issues raised. Through discussion, people share ideas about problems and together they formulate solutions to them. More often than not, this is not enough. The College strongly believes that unless education leads to organized action, it is wasteful and has lost its mission. The discussions generate action on the part of club members to improve their conditions. The special columns created for farmers on farming for instance, generated interest among young and old farmers alike to take to serious farming and adopt modern farming techniques (Opare-Abetia, 1972).

Some specific examples on actions taken by the Anfoeta Readers' Club will suffice for the purpose of this discussion:

Members of the Readers' Club at Anfoeta read and discussed an article on food production and preservation in *Kpodoga* in 1996. After the discussion, club members requested the Department of Social Welfare to teach them how to preserve their foodstuffs. The staff of the Department from Ho honoured the invitation and organized workshops on food preservation for them. The majority of members who attended these workshops claimed that they have been preserving their food satisfactorily since then. On reading the articles on communal labour and town cleaning campaigns the Anfoeta Readers' Club has regularly conducted clean-up campaigns in their communities and markets.

The Anfoeta Readers' Club continues to be one of the active clubs in the circulation zone of *Kpodoga*. It has a total membership of 120 people. The local organizer, Victor Agbleze, is committed to making everyone in his village literate. Some have started communal farming and doormat making as a result of what they learnt from the paper and from functional literacy programmes.

Content Role of Kpodoga

Agriculture is the main concern of the people in the area covered by *Kpodoga*. *Kpodoga,* therefore, reports on new and better ways of producing food. The rural newspaper further helps improve the daily lives of people in every respect

Theories of Community Education 71

— social, cultural, economic and political. Stories in *Kpodoga* thus deal with self-help, health, literacy, school and church activities as well as wildlife, sports and government.

By 1990, the majority of grown-ups had developed interest in adult education activities. Many people could now appreciate the need for lifelong education and the importance of being able to read and write. They were anxious to see the rural newspaper's coverage area expanded to communities where it had not yet reached. At the same time, the Institute of Adult Education had joined in the world discussion of population growth and had embarked upon a programme of providing population education for Ghanaians. *Kpodoga* has accordingly, since 1994, increased its volume to eight pages with four pages remaining a general newspaper while the additional four are devoted to population issues and the environment.

Radio broadcasts are used to increase the teaching effectiveness of the community newspaper, *Kpodoga*. A partnership was formed with the Rural Broadcast Department of the Ghana Broadcasting Corporation in 1977. The newspaper staffs were responsible for preparing the educational materials and organizing recording sessions with the *Kpodoga* Readers' Clubs. These were published in the newspaper and discussed after the radio broadcast. The activity that was started with success, unfortunately, stopped when the Radio Producer was transferred from the Ho District to the GBC Headquarters in Accra.

Kpodoga editorials on topical issues, letters to the editor, and obituaries, humorous strips and interviews with local personalities make the paper popular, educative and very interesting. Spaces between articles are filled with proverbial sayings that encourage hard work and honesty and reflect local culture and popular beliefs.

Although the rural community press may concentrate on issues relevant to its low-income community, it has expanded its scope by letting people know who their neighbours are and what kind of experiences and achievements they are also going through. As a result, the higher literate class and urban communities are taking keener interest in it than before.
The editorial role of the rural newspaper is, according to the editor Aduamah (Ideas and Actions No. 141, FAO, Rome, 1981)

> ... strikingly different from that of the Ghanaian national press and the Western press after which it is patterned. Objectivity of reporting and article selection according to what will sell the largest number of papers is the long established foundations of the Western press and those that follow their example.
>
> But while objective communication is successful with the high literate classes,

it may fail lamentably with the new literate rural folk who are not yet able to read with complete understanding and who assume the written word to be infallible.

Indeed, the content of the rural newspaper is set in an African background with local activities, history, proverbs, anecdotes and story telling which are native to the African. These help the reader to think faster and find facts for himself as he finds himself exposed to the realities of life. In the process of reflecting on the articles in the newspaper readers see the need for change. They, therefore, start discussing seriously about change. In their discussions they consider various alternatives available for the solution of specific problems. In making decisions, they prioritize the alternatives. They no longer continue repeating the same processes in doing things. Changes occur in the lives of people.

The Demonstration Farm, Tsawenu

Introduction
As it has been pointed out, there is clear evidence that the people of Awudome area are, in the main, farmers who till the land to make a living (Opare-Abetia, 1980). In that respect, the prime concern for an integrated development programme is agriculture. A particularly noteworthy aspect of this programme is the Demonstration Farm, which is essentially the core of the entire project.

The farm started in 1970/71 when a ten-acre plot of land at Tsawenu in the Awudome Traditional Area was acquired from the Agbenya family of Anyirawase on very liberal terms. The importance of this farm cannot be over-estimated. The demonstration farm serves as a training centre for the people and as the basis for economic and social development. This is because adult education for social change for primary producers should concern itself with the development of the economic activity of the people.

The importance of agriculture in rural development has also been emphasized by Coombs and Ahmed (1974) when they noted, "once agricultural development is firmly under way, the process spreads to other economic sectors". It is believed that if farmers produce enough food to feed themselves and sell the surplus and raw materials, the effect will spread to other sectors of the economy. The farmer will make new demands. As a result, artisans, craftsmen, and shopkeepers will also have the stimulus and markets in the area will boom with activity. The system in Ghana, however, is that, when farmers produce more, there is a glut on the market. The main economic factors are semi-processing of products and marketing. Education thus becomes an essential component of the agricultural revolution.

There is yet another reason why there is the need for the development

Theories of Community Education 73

of agriculture as a necessary component of the Awudome Integrated Rural Development Programme. Until recently, work on the land was considered by the youth and the educated as an occupation for illiterates. Land was then becoming a dwindling asset. The school drop-outs, school left-outs and school leavers were not trained to work with their hands. The promise, which the schools held for them to become white-collar job workers, had become fantasies. The formal education system is seen by many people as an institution mainly for frustration, imagination and hallucination at the end of the day.

Many critics of the school system especially the deschoolers like Illich (1971) and Reimer (1971) called for the overhauling of the school system. They would wish the schools to be community-based and more responsive to community vocations and societal needs. Agriculture, which is the main occupation of people in the rural areas, must be given the appropriate attention in the educational curriculum.

The schools, the critics believe, have failed to produce graduates to suitably fit into society. Many of the school leavers and drop-outs are found in the streets roaming about for jobs, which are not available. Their parents also support them to look for the "whiteman's job", since this will justify their investments in educating them. However, the jobs are not sufficiently available.

Existing realities include the fact that raw materials are needed for industries, people are hungry, and fertile lands are available for farming, while some of the youth are idle and frustrated. Schools and educational institutions and society in general are, therefore, called upon by the deschoolers to fund training programmes, which can make people fit into the modern productive system of the community. It is in view of these demands that educational authorities are trying to embrace the idea of making agriculture a necessary component of the school curriculum.

A target population for the Demonstration Farm are the young school leavers who have not acquired any skills and cannot be employed. They are brought back to school on the farm and helped to learn to stay on the land. Students of the Tsito Junior Secondary School do their agricultural practical work on the farm to be equipped with farming skills. One of such programmes for Tsito Junior Secondary School is reported below.

Linking School with Environment

For an outing, the staff of the Tsito Awudome Junior Secondary School took their final year students to participate in a workshop on the Demonstration Farm at Tsito. The students learnt about vegetable cultivation and the proper use and maintenance of simple farm tools. They discussed problems related to production and marketing of their products.

The one-day non-formal education programme was full of animated discussions in which "school involvement in community activities was high." The Junior Secondary School was, according to the Tsito Headteacher, Mr. A. K. Adzei, introduced among other reasons "to inculcate in students an appropriate attitude towards manual work and to prepare them for the world of work." (*People's Daily Graphic*, Accra, January 26, 1987).

Women and men are also actively involved in training programmes on the farm. They have seriously embarked upon vegetable growing which is not common in the community. To win the economic war against poverty, farmers undertake small-scale farming especially beans growing, backyard goat and sheep rearing and poultry keeping.

These farmers exchange ideas about modern methods of farming. They learn to plant in rows, use the appropriate fertilizer, fertilize crops on time and learn modern farm maintenance practices. The course content for farmers is not centered on agriculture alone. Poverty is discussed. This draws the farmers into the new economic and social system. Sometimes, they become aware that their poverty is not due to super-natural forces but to their ignorance and at times to the existing social and economic structures. They also learn to relate well with neighbours and to communicate better with them.

Through the implementation of new farming techniques, it is learnt that poverty can be alleviated and that the farmer can liberate himself from ignorance. Many of these old-time farmers are converted to the new faith of modern practices for higher yields. The farmers including the youth now begin to realize the fact that land is the greatest resource and that there is much money in the soil. They, therefore, start serious work in the cultivation of the land.

The farmers are encouraged not to cultivate more acres than they can maintain. In other words, they are to cultivate the acreage they can manage conveniently. They learn about mixed farming, specially, how maize, beans, yam and cassava can be inter-cropped and how to keep animals and bees. They are also advised to form co-operatives to liberate themselves from want, and on the advice of the College, the Awudome Women Farmers' Co-operative has been formed.

Awudome Women Farmers Co-operative
Coombs and Ahmed (1974) expressed concern about the neglect of women farmers in the agricultural sector even though women play useful roles in this sector. They emphasized that "it is important to stress the serious neglect of the rural female audience by agricultural extension services".

The involvement of women in the agricultural sector is very important. This is because when men clear the farmland, it is the African women who are responsible for the planting, weeding, harvesting, preparation, preservation and marketing of the food. The main occupation of African women is farming.

Also, women generally play useful roles in society. The mother is the first teacher to the child in the family. As the child grows, it is the responsibility of the woman to train and nurture him. As the child grows into adulthood, it is the woman who trains him. As the adult becomes disabled in old age, it is the woman who takes care of him. In addition, it is the woman who takes care of household duties and if there is no food in the house, the woman has to manage to feed the family. The Awudome woman is a petty trader, farmer, and member of religious and social groups. Yet, she is not given enough formal and non-formal educational opportunities to cope with her responsibilities.

In view of the above, the integrated project initiated the formation of Awudome Women Farmers Co-operative in 1985. This is an organization of women drawn from all the Awudome towns. Membership of the Co-operative increased from 20 to 28 within a six-month period after registration. The total membership as at the close of 1997 was 45 (Farm Organizer's Report, 97). The women, regularly, participate in workshops on the farm and have been given a portion of the farmland at Tsawenu for cultivation. The process enables staff to look more closely at the farming practices of local farmers. The women also readily compare their methods with those of the staff and correct their mistakes.

The public health division of the Ministry of Health has been attracted into the programme to support the women in the preparation and preservation of food. This component of food processing and preparation has become one of the popular aspects of the women's programme on the farm. Human relations workshops are also organized for them in the workshop session. They usually discuss the various aspects of family life education and reproductive health. Issues relating to prostitution and its attendant hazards are discussed. Other components of the programme include planning, management, budgeting, storage and harvesting of crops.

A major problem was that initially the women viewed the project as a welfare service and expected free meals, pesticides, and transport fares from the staff of the project. Through constant education, they shifted from this dependency attitude towards self-reliance. The women have now come to accept the fact that only they themselves could initiate the process of changing their "poor" situation (*African Farming,* March/April 1988). They learn to cultivate crops, take care of the crops, plan and take responsibility over their lives. Survival strategies are thus worked with this silent working group. Some of them have started serious farming with good results. Others also claim that they can plan their budget better. Their men counterparts have got the ideas from the women to start serious farming especially, the cultivation of beans, which has become very popular in Awudome now.

Liberal Education Programmes on the Farm
Liberal education programmes in the form of debates are also organized by the staff of *Kpodoga* and the Demonstration Farm. The debates usually take place on the demonstration plot. The first in the series of such debates was on bush burning. This was to draw farmers' attention to the hazards of bush burning and environmental degradation. The debate was covered by the *Daily Graphic* in its issue of December 3, 1985 and the Rural Newspaper, *Kpodoga*.

According to the *Daily Graphic* report "the debaters who were in favour of bush burning were only reduced to making the sweeping statement that they supported bush burning because it makes grazing, planting, and hunting easier." Voting in the end of the debate showed that two were in favour of continuous bush burning, 28 against and there were 10 abstentions.

Winners of the debate marched through town carrying placards with messages, "Save the Forest for Your Children," "Save the Forest and Save a Life." Education on environmental protection was carried across from the farm to the town. The rate of bush burning has reduced remarkably since these debates began. The debates have become an annual activity. Farmers are always reminded of the dangers of bush burning. In the recent past, no outbreak of bush fires has been recorded in the community.

The bitter controversy over leaving sheep, goats and poultry loose to roam about and graze indiscriminately in African villages still rages on. At Tsawenu, however, debates have been held over the issue at which nearly all aspects of the problem were reviewed. The debates, which have been reported in the *African Farming* magazine, were organized by the Institute of Adult Education and the Ministry of Agriculture, for farmer groups.

Firstly, the debates gave the animal rearers, food crop farmers, gardeners and market traders a clearer understanding of the extent of the usefulness of animals. Secondly, attention was focused on the very real possibility of increasing production through education. Thirdly, participants learnt to keep animals in a business-like manner. Animals are not to be let loose to fend for themselves. Comparisons were made between traditional and modern practices of animal rearing. Finally, advantages and disadvantages of both practices were drawn (*African Farming*, London, 1991). As a result, the majority of the farmers have begun to keep their animals in a more business-like manner. They feed them on fodder and pen them during farming seasons.

The Impact of the Farm on Awudome

A new dimension of the farm work is the introduction of new crops into the Awudome area. The farm introduced the growing of exotic seeds such as radish, carrot, lettuce and cabbage to the community in January/February 1986. The college popularized the improved maize "Dobidi" from the Agricultural Research Institute at Kwadaso and an improved variety of cowpea IT 82E-16 in the community in May, 1986. The farm did not only introduce these crops but organized workshops to educate farmers on cultural practices connected with them. As a result, many farmers in the community now cultivate these brands of maize and cowpea in preference to the local ones whose yields are very low. Because of the success of the experiment in the development of the vegetables, a farmer from Nkwanta started serious farming in these exotic plants on the banks of Tsawe stream very close to the Demonstration Farm.

Another new activity is the development of vegetable and palm fruit nurseries. Experiments in those ventures have proved encouraging and have become a permanent feature in the farm programmes. Nursery practices are demonstrated to farmers on the raising of vegetables. Peppers, onion, tomatoes, garden-egg seedlings so raised are sold to the public. Vegetable growing has, therefore, become popular among Awudome farmers. Workshops on palm cultivation are often reported on the national radio.

In the early 1980s, the College was excited to introduce bullock ploughs into the Awudome community to provide some respite for farmers who relied mainly on the use of hoes and cutlasses. A farmhand from the Demonstration Farm received training in animal traction from the Northern Region. Local farmers expressed their reservation about the survival of bullocks in an area infested with tsetseflies. But the College did not take the advice of these farmers. The flies disturbed the bullocks. As a result, the bullocks died a few months on arrival from Yendi. We learnt our lesson: the farmers were not taken into partnership in the introduction of bullock ploughs.

Workshops are the tools by which the Demonstration Farm disseminates its educational ideas to its clientele. The College is always mindful of Sophocle's advice (400 BC) at workshops that: "one must learn by doing the thing; for though you may think you know it, you have no certainty until you try". At the workshops, farmers take part not only in discussion, but also in practical demonstration, handling spraying machines, planting and applying fertilizer to the crops. They must all try to prove their competence by handling the farm equipment. One by one, participants demonstrate what they learn. According to the farm manager who does extension work, many of the techniques learnt on the farm are transferred to individual farms adequately.

It is also believed that workshops are not enough to help young farmers settle successfully or other farmers to work comfortably in the field. Extension visits are made to farms which include those of the schools in Awudome, Dzento's garden-egg farm at Avenui, Megaga's oil palm plantation, Dzirentsi's cowpea farm, 31st December Women's Farm, Anyirawase and Badu's palm plantation in Tsito. These farms have been established in response to training received on the Demonstration Farm. The clientele have also been introduced to banks for loans which some could not have access to, for the years past (ARAC, 1996).

In 1997, approaches were made to the Ministry of Agriculture's Irrigation Department for the construction of a dam with shallow tube wells for irrigation of the Demonstration Farm for all year round vegetable gardening. Preliminary studies have been conducted for the project. The irrigated plot was to be divided into smallholder units and allocated mainly to members of the Awudome Women Farmers' Association (ARAC, 1997). Currently, programmes undertaken include the development of mango, cashew and palm nurseries. In addition to the educational component of the project, the seedlings are sold to farmers for cultivation (ARAC, 1998).

The management staff of the farm have discovered that growth stagnates if it is isolated. It therefore, makes serious collaborative efforts with other agricultural institutions to plan programmes and share ideas. Some of these institutions include the Adventist Development and Relief Agency (ADRA), the Grains Development Board (GDB), the then Volta Region Agricultural Development Project (VORADEP) and the Ministry of Agriculture.

As it has been discussed above, the farm programmes have met with some success. "Some individual farmers have adopted some of the crops and techniques which they resisted earlier and seem to be happy that they did so" (Opare-Abetia, 1980:12). The same report noted that the agricultural programmes expanded the outlook of farmers and these have led to an increase in production in some cases. Many of the farmers contacted, admitted that they found workshops on the farm and improved types of seedlings useful. In an interview with the supervisor of the farm, it became evident that the farm has made significant landmarks during its 30 years of operation (1970–2000). Available records prepared by the supervisor illustrated some of the achievements of the farm as mentioned below.

Palm plantations, which people believe, would not do well in the area have become popular among farmers. At the close of 2000, at least 30 farmers had developed their own small-scale palm plantations. As many as 45 farmers are also engaged in small-scale vegetable (tomatoes, pepper, okro, cabbage) farming. Mushroom farming is also catching up fast in the area with 18 farmers actively engaged in it. Cultivation of maize and other crops is undertaken by many farmers in the community adopting modern methods of farm management like planting on time and in rows, using insecticides, constructing appropriate barns, managing their crops regularly, treating their crops before storage and marketing them at the right time.

The majority of the farmers are gradually moving from the subsistence level to the market economy. It would, however, be too optimistic to expect that great changes in the agricultural sector of the community would occur immediately. The signs, however, indicate the hope that with the appropriate education given at the Farm, changes would come, but slowly.

Emerging Issues

The first step in planning the integrated community education programme was a workshop at Tsito, which discussed The Problem of Development. At this conference, a branch of the PEA was officially formed and the decision was taken to build an educational centre. With sacrifice, dedication and commitment from all stakeholders of the project, the Awudome Integrated Rural Development Programme was established.

The adult education establishment in Awudome has been working with different types of groups. These include the Boys' Scouts, tailors and seamstresses, Awudome Women's Association, the various *Kpodoga* Readers' Clubs, the PEA and the Ho District Assembly. With some of the groups it is a problem of improving the chance of marketability or obtaining credit or linking their small enterprises with the operations of the larger centralized enterprises.

Leadership and revenue mobilization courses are organized for groups as appropriate. Demonstrations are organized on new and better ways of producing food using the traditional tools such as the hoe and the cutlass.

Characteristics of Awudome Project
Generally speaking, the characteristics of Awudome Project do not differ remarkably from those of its sister Folk High Schools in the Nordic countries. Local conditions and changes in programme demands have, however, influenced the characteristics in ARAC.

Like the Folk High Schools, the College seeks to offer its facilities and services to as many people as possible. Long-term courses are, therefore, not encouraged. This allows for the running of different types of courses for the benefit of many people.

Courses are tailor-made to suit the needs of various occupational and professional groups. These tailor-made courses are meant to equip individuals with skills and knowledge that can be immediately used for living. The education provided is not the "diploma disease" type of education whereby students feverishly learn irrelevant theories just to pass their examinations. The programmes are combined with work experiences. If certificates are awarded at the end of courses, they are certificates of attendance specifying the types of courses provided.

The role of the integrated project in enhancing women's participation in programmes is also emphasized. It was for this reason that the Institute of Adult Education appointed a woman organizer in the persons of Miss Jessie Kumah in 1987 and Miss Magdalene Kofituo in 1993 to organize programmes for Awudome women. They mobilized the women in town cleaning and community development projects like construction of a kindergarten. Women are, therefore, always with men at workshops or participating in workshops organized for them alone.

The community education project at Tsito does not attach much importance to paper qualifications as entry requirements. By so doing, it mobilizes all the potential contributors to development. Both literates and illiterates have equal chances to learn and improve upon their quality of life and contribute to community development. Indeed, the majority of people trained on the farm and those who take the courses organized for the local community are illiterate. Because of this, the local language of the community, that is Ewe, is used to conduct the face-to-face encounters.

A serious attempt is also made to promote the culture of the local people. This is demonstrated in the involvement of the traditional rulers, cultural and choral groups in educational and course programmes. The local communication channels are also used in the educational process.

The Folk High Schools and the ARAC believe in organizing programmes for small numbers. Usually, the intake is for small numbers. This allows for the forging of closer links among participants.

It would be quite absurd to duplicate for adults the kind of educational experiences to which children are exposed. An adult college is thus meant to give the adult participant quite a new educational outlook in terms of teaching and learning, environment and facilitator — participant relationships. The environment is to suit adult learners so that they will be able to use the skills learnt immediately in the development process.

An important characteristic of the project is its openness to and attraction of all categories of adults from their work places and situations. There are some businessmen, administrators, parents and even the unemployed who because of the nature of their work or some circumstances cannot reflect on their work and life, take stock of them and plan new strategies for personal and group development. This is one of the main reasons to justify the existence of residential adult education institutions. People need to have time to look back, evaluate their existing situations and work. They will then be in a better position to plan well for the future.

The College does extension work through the Demonstration Farm, *Kpodoga* and liberal education programmes. It runs this integrative rural development programme in collaboration with other departments and groups. But usually, participants, collaborators and facilitators who are scattered all over the community, are brought together into residence at the College. This is done to justify the College's existence as a residential adult college.

Programmes organized under the project have their distinctive features in terms of course content, facilitator-learner relationships, and relaxed general atmosphere during workshops and relationship between the college and the community. A series of short programmes are organized to satisfy different tastes.

Educational Methodology Used Under the Integrated Community Programme
Until recently, educated people used to arrive at the Adult College courses with memories of the British adult education tradition that stresses the lecture or recitation method.

On arrival for the first stages of courses, participants expected to see printed programmes showing day-to-day activities, an orderly lecture hall with seats arranged row by row, with lecturers who knew, presenting facts, and participants who did not know, taking notes.

But course organizers had, since the early 1980s, been using the psychosocial method that adopts the philosophy of Paulo Freire as its basis. In this movement, the emphasis is on learning through activity and interest. The interests, needs, and problems of learners, rather than subject matter, are thought to be the proper focus for the organization of the learning process. Gone are the days when the learner was thought to be a mere passive receiver to be filled, as a petrol engine might be filled or activated, with petrol.

It is usually quite difficult for most participants, in their early experience with the psychosocial methods, to put aside their own preconceptions of what needs to be taught. As the courses progress, however, they soon feel that there are alternative ways of teaching by which such social vices as prostitution, smuggling, embezzlement of public funds and tribalism can be eliminated from society. They feel that a programme prepared in advance could not have succeeded equally with them all.

Course participants are adults with different characteristics and they come from different places and for different reasons, which they express like: "I am an extension officer, I want to learn how to motivate people and to sustain their interest." "I am a chief, I expect the course to explain how to enlist the active participation of people." Other participants expect the workshops to show them how to work with seniors, how to use different methods of approach in leading people. Others still come to see how people try to solve problems similar to theirs. The self-presentations and ensuing discussions produce an overall picture of the origins, structures, activities and problems of participants.

Courses proceed to draw a timetable to satisfy the expressed demands of participants. For course organizers and facilitators, the absence of a programme prepared in advance could allow them to judge the seriousness and purposefulness of participants by seeing what issues they take up for discussions.

Courses at the College at Tsito and on the Demonstration Farm at Tsawenu provide opportunities for sharing experiences of many sorts. Participants have the freedom to talk, listen and work together in groups and in committees. Physical exercises, outings, debates, games, sing-songs, story telling, drawing and picture discussion, picking up of name tags and pinning them to the owners' shirts, and other play acts are designed to encourage active and flexible interaction with facilitators. Both facilitators and learners, at times together and at other times in turn, handle tools and equipment to take part in demonstrations. Participants break into small groups and meet again in the larger group, or just turn to their neighbours and buzz with them. Eventually, the shy ones are also willing to talk.

Course leaders are members of staff of the Institute of Adult Education. Some of them travel from other stations to join their colleagues at Tsito. In order to pool resources together, the Institute sometimes organizes courses in collaboration with other sector departments, agencies, institutions and organizations. At the end of many workshops, participant draw action plans to be implemented on their return to their work places and communities.

The experiences gained at Tsito and Tsawenu deserve to be widely known. And here the *Kpodoga* newspaper is always in the position of extending the activities and experiences beyond the university centres at Tsito and Tsawenu.

Problems
There are many challenges facing the Awudome integrated rural development project. In the first place, the Awudome community has been complaining about the limited number of programmes mounted for them in view of their

immense contributions towards the construction of the College. Such a concern may be justified in the way and manner it is expressed. The College administration can, therefore, revive the College Board of Administration including local leaders, to plan a more systematic course programme for the local community.

In the second place, *Kpodoga* has been running into publication problems. It is irregular and the production level has dropped. There is always a shortage of chemicals, newsprint, supporting staff and lack of transport. Its main problem is the lack of printing facilities in the rural area. Even at a time when so much is being said about decentralization, the newspaper's manuscripts have to be taken down south 140 kilometers for word processing, typesetting and printing at the national capital, Accra. The long distance makes the supervision of the typesetting difficult for the Editor, proofreading cumbersome and typographical errors unavoidable. The newspaper which started in 1976 with donations of a car, newsprint and chemicals by UNESCO, had by 1986 dropped its print-run from 5,000 to 2,000 copies, though the size was increased from four to eight pages.

In the third place, despite Ghana government's recognition of the singular contribution, which the College, the farmer education at Twawenu and the newspaper are making to social and economic life in general, it has not been able to give enough financial support to expand college infrastructure. The master plan, pending available grants to be undertaken, includes the provision of modern kitchen, additional classrooms, senior and junior staff quarters and printing facilities. But in the present economic circumstances there is very little hope of obtaining adequate government funds for implementing the plan.

In the fourth place, nothing has been heard about the bullock ploughs since the bullocks died on the farm. The farmers have reverted to the use of hoes and cutlasses. The challenge for the Institute is to revisit its method of land preparation for crops.

Impact of the Integrated Community Education Programme
Despite the problems facing the educational programmes of the College, it has contributed greatly to overall betterment of the material situation of the people of Awudome and its environs. Since the start of the programme in 1950, many changes have taken place. We cannot, for instance, refer to Tsito now as a village as it has lost its air of monotony, boredom and bleak poverty, and has put on prettiness with running water, electric lights and access roads. Community Education explains a lot of this change. Today, Awudome can be singled out in the area as a model of what a farming community could be in terms of self-reliance, hardwork and appropriate ideology. It has come to lead

the way in crop diversification. Attempts have been made to introduce new vegetables like cabbage. More cash crops are being grown such as oil palm and cropping patterns are changing for the better. Mushroom growing and bee keeping are common in the area. Today, the people of Awudome can afford to eat diet better than before.

The programmes have enabled the rural people to become interested in reading newspapers. *Kpodoga* has given the opportunity to many people to make enquiries and to seek information generally from wherever they can get it. Every village, even if it does not excel, wants it to be reported in the *Kpodoga* that it is undertaking some community development project. It may be a communal cleaning of village gutters beside which women sell prepared foods. It may be the building of a clinic, a market, or a latrine. In this way, the community education programme has succeeded in motivating communities to organize themselves and take group action.

A challenge, which *Kpodoga* has taken up since the early 1990s, is to provide reproductive health education to the community. And this must have been helping the young people to prevent sexual problems and improve their reproductive health. The emphasis now is on HIV/AIDS education. *Kpodoga* has made the reading and writing of Ewe language popular. People in the *Kpodoga* circulation zone are, therefore, patronizing literacy classes provided by the Non-Formal Education Division so that they can also read the paper and contribute news items for publication.

Apart from the material benefits offered by the programme, the community education efforts have also succeeded in raising people's consciousness and in increasing their awareness and participation in decision-making. By virtue of the nature of courses organized by the college, the people of Awudome Traditional Area have been exposed to people and new ideas from all over Ghana and from almost all the continents of the world. This has created a constant source of informal education for the local Awudome people to improve their way of life and work. Their interest in sporting and cultural activities has been aroused and sustained over the years.

Conclusions

The Awudome Residential Adult College (ARAC) is unique in several respects. It started as a Folk High School but with a shift from the main Nordic Folk High School objectives. Whereas the Nordic schools focused on the promotion of nationalism, ARAC focused on personal and skill development though slight references to nationalism were made. It was built through the joint effort of the Awudome community, the Institute of Adult Education, the PEA, Denmark and a host of local and international organizations. It continues to work closely with the community in which it has been established. It has become a powerhouse for the training of farmers, women, youth leaders traditional rulers, traditional birth attendants and people from all walks of life.

As a result of the establishment of the College at Tsito, Tsito has assumed a prominent position, in terms of development, among Awudome towns and its neighbours. It shows how education can enhance the development of a community since her citizens are more exposed to new ideas, both local and international.

The College believes that salvation for the Ghanaian is something to achieve but not just something to hope for. The College, therefore, opens its doors for and offers its advisory services to the poor, the illiterate and the unemployed. They become aware of their problems and adopt strategies to solve them. They, therefore, become happy when they solve their own problems. The results of the capacity building programmes of the College then emphasize the point that a happy community is not the product of chance but of appropriate community education, careful programme planning and timely effective action.

The College with the limited facilities available has been playing its part to satisfy some local, national and international demands. But like all human institutions, the College cannot satisfactorily meet all demands, nor can it pretend that its philosophy and practice have been in the right direction all the time. As a university institution, *inter alia*, it is to research and experiment. When the experiment is successful, it is then sold to the larger society. *Kpodoga* and the Demonstration Farm have proved to be useful institutions in the general development process which can be replicated in communities as the media of information and education and vehicles for development. These can be initiated by communities and sponsored by district assemblies and non-governmental organizations.

The Awudome community education practice, a necessary component of adult education in its small ways, looks forward like a small candle with its gentle flames, to give light and hope to many people in the development process.

Chapater 4

COMPARISON OF COMMUNITY EDUCATION EXPERIMENTS IN DENMARK, CANADA, BRITAIN AND GHANA

Introduction

In this final chapter, observations on the issues raised are made and conclusions drawn on the origins and implementation of community education programmes discussed in the previous chapters. Some of the theoretical basis that shaped the practice are also discussed. Other areas covered include the common trends in the practice of community education.

Origins

The background of communities in the four countries necessitating the introduction of community education was almost similar. In all the four countries, social and economic problems existed. In Canada, farmers, fishermen and workers in general in Antigonish were living under poor conditions. There was a decline in agricultural activities as residents drifted into the urban areas. The same difficulties faced farmers and fishermen in Denmark. The fate of workers was worsened in Denmark by the German invasion which weakened the economic base of workers in the wake of political instability.

In Britain, residents of the new settlement in Leigh Park were experiencing difficult social and economic situations as many of them were unemployed in their new environment. There was the need in all these communities for the social and economic integration of the people into the main stream of development. By and large, relations in the Western communities of this study may be classified as those in the *Gesellschaft*.

Unlike the communities in the Western countries discussed above, the Awudome community in Ghana has a unique traditional political structure and cultural values. Traditional forms of worship, economic activity, political administration and social justice have prevailed. Farming, the main occupation of the people, is at the subsistence level. The people cannot, therefore, make ends meet. Relationships in the Awudome state have been primary and people participate daily in communal activities. It is comparable to the *Gemeinschaft*.

Theories of Community Education Used

Breakthrough Strategy

An important tool in arousing community interest in community work and education is an appropriate breakthrough strategy. In all the programmes discussed in previous chapters a variety of strategies had been used. In the three Western experiments, no invitation was sent by residents to the community educators to come to their aid. In the Ghanaian situation, the community extended invitations to the community educators to come to their aid. In the four experiments, however, breakthrough strategies were almost the same. The community educators identified themselves with the aspirations of community members. They undertook needs assessment exercises among the people through visits, public meetings, open fora, speeches and distribution of leaflets. They were able to draw people's attention to participate in the programmes. They also built strong relationships with communities and especially, with community leaders. In the Danish experiment, Grundtvig went further to use songs and sermons to conscientize people while in the British experiment, Fordham and his colleagues utilized theatre performances to break the apathetic stance of people.

Model of Community Education Used

The choice of the model of community education depends largely on the objectives set by the community educators to achieve. In all the cases under study, the main objective of the educators was to liberate people from social discomfort and economic hardship. It was against this background that the education favoured and implemented the liberating model of community education. A friendly environment was created by the educators for communities to develop their potentials.

In the Denmark, Canada and Ghana experiments, farmers were organized and trained to actively engage in their occupations. They were taught new methods of farming. Agricultural co-operatives were formed especially in Denmark, Ghana and Canada for production, consumption and marketing not only of food crops but also other agricultural products. Fishermen in Canada could also boast of strong fishermen's co-operatives which gave them strong bargaining powers in the markets. The economic status and the lifestyle of all these agricultural co-operatives improved greatly. As it was pointed out, the farmers in the Ghana experiment could eat better diet than before. In Britain, the manpower and job creation scheme accessed jobs for the unemployed youth after they were given the necessary training and counseling.

On the social front, opportunities and facilities were provided to participants to join functional community groups to promote their own interest and entertainment activities. In Denmark and Canada youth groups, lecture societies and agricultural co-operatives were not only occupational societies but also social groups. Danish music tradition dated from this era. In Ghana, music and cultural groups and sporting associations were formed to provide entertainment and relaxation to members. In Britain, Focus 230 provided facilities to Single Parent Family Groups, Holiday Play Scheme, the Deaf Club and Working Men's Group to plan and enjoy their own social activities. Residents were liberated from boredom, which existed in the community before the community education was initiated.

Typology of Community Education Adopted

In all the experiments discussed above, the typology of the community practice extensively adopted was the "Adult Education for the Community". A prepackaged form of education has not been imposed on the communities. The occupations and the social needs of the beneficiaries have been identified in collaboration with the people. Beneficiaries were taken into partnership in the implementation of the programmes. What the community educators succeeded in doing was to create a friendly environment and provide appropriate education to motivate beneficiaries to learn and work. Community educators remained catalysts in the education and development process while beneficiaries remained active participants working to improve their own situations. The programmes were community-oriented type of adult education. Taking the learning opportunities to people in their environment helped to boost their ego. Anchoring them in familiar setting increased their confidence.

Approaches and Methodologies

A number of approaches and methodologies were adopted in the implementation of the programmes to ensure success and sustainability. Some of these approaches are discussed below:

Community Entry Approach
One of the first important approaches adopted in all the experiments was the community entry approach discussed earlier on under the Breakthrough Strategy. Community educators through visits, dialogue and negotiations were able to establish rapport with participants. They fraternised with participants and identified themselves with the development aspirations of participants. Participants also identified their own problems, planned their own lines of action and came to the realization that the programmes were their own and

their successful implementation was in their own interest. This sense of ownership of the projects by community members sustained their interest in the projects. Participants appreciated this bottom-up approach to community education.

Leadership Training
Leadership training was found to be a very important feature of community education. This is because the success of any programme depends on the quality and efficiency of its leadership. Local leaders take over the responsibilities of educators in case of the latters' withdrawal when the programme is officially completed. Leaders need to acquire special skills so that they can be in control and direct the course of the group. It is for these reasons that leadership training programmes became necessary features of the various programmes.

Leaders of the various groups in each community programme were trained according to the skills they needed to organize their groups. In Denmark, teachers and former students of Folk High Schools, were trained to take up positions in their communities, local government councils, and different types of organizations as leaders. In Ghana leadership-training programmes were mounted not only for the various units of the programme but also for other organizations such as youth groups and government departments. The trained leaders took over management component of the programme at the various community and unit levels. It is noted that leadership training has become an annual feature on the calendar of the Canada experiment.

Literacy Education
Literacy is a necessary tool for the development process. Participants must learn to read and write what they learn to ensure clear understanding, easy referencing and accurate implementation of lessons learnt. They must learn to calculate figures so that their customers and creditors do not cheat them. For these reasons, literacy education was attached to all the programmes. Study circles were established in the various communities to constitute classes for the literacy programmes. In some cases as it were in Canada and Denmark, occupational groups such as farmers and fishermen became study circles. Community newspapers such as *The Extension Bulletin* in Canada, the *Kpodoga* in Ghana and *The Leap* in Britain were established to provide reading materials to study circles. In Canada and Britain library services were provided to the learners.

Motivation
Another important strategy promoted was the provision of motivation to learners to sustain their interest. Motivational techniques such as regular visits and inspiring speeches to participants to improve upon their conditions were made. Sporting, music, cultural and entertainment activities did not only bring participants together but also kept their morale high to continue to perform creditably. People were encouraged to achieve success in the work they did and realized tangible benefit in the form of material benefits including food crop and handicrafts. Another source of motivation was the creation of opportunities to participants to freely discuss issues and to undertake occupations they were familiar with. Almost all the participants learnt and worked happily in a friendly familiar environment.

Use of Structures and Networks
It would have been difficult for the community educators to work single-handed with the various groups. They, therefore, encouraged the formation of structures or groups in the communities where they operated. They also networked with other organizations with similar working action plans and objectives. In Britain, the project team collaborated with the Workers' Educational Association, the British Association of Settlements, and Local Education Authority. The Ghana experiment collaborated with the Ministry of Agriculture, Ghana Broadcasting Corporation, the University of Ghana and the Ho District Assembly, among others. All these organizations pooled their resources together to promote and sustain the programmes.

Role of Animateurs/Community Educators

Animateurs/community educators in the programmes contributed to the success of the activities undertaken. The dedication and commitment of the initiators and the educators of the programmes were commendable. In Denmark, the commitment of Grundtvig, Nielson and Laub led to the initiation of the consolidation and sustainability of the programme. So also did the dedication of Mcpherson, Father Coady and MacDonald lead to the success story of the Canada experiment. In the British experiment, the commitment of Fordham and his colleagues contributed to the viability of the programme. The moral and material support of Kimble, Greenstreet and the College staff coupled with their enthusiasm in making the programme succeed accounted for the growth and sustainability of the programme.

Content and Context of Community Adult Education

Community education adopts holistic approach to curriculum development. It is an integrated type of programme which incorporates all disciplines to cater for the needs and interests of different categories of people in the community. Some of the subjects treated were agriculture (fishing and farming) health care and health education, political education, moral and cultural education. In the area of entertainment, sporting, music and leisure activities have been organized as appropriate. The programmes have been organized for the youth and adults of both sexes. There were no cultural or gender biases eliminating any group of people from the programmes.

Conclusion

Some theories and practices in community education programmes by four institutions have been visited. These were the Folk High Schools in Denmark, the Antigonish Movement in Canada, the Leigh Park Communities Project in Britain and Awudome Integrated Community Project in Ghana. These programmes were initiated and implemented by committed community educators whose visions to make communities functional materialized.

The basic principles and fundamental requirements of community education and community participation featured prominently in all the experiments. Community education facilitated voluntary mobilization of people in familiar environments. Organized community members in familiar environments reflected on their needs, interests, aspirations, concerns and values. In the decision-making process, group members defined their goals, and planned strategies to ensure sustainable and equitable development. The collective decision taken bound them together to take action to improve their conditions. Action was self-generated and gave the opportunity to all to access productive resources and social services. Participation enhanced the improvement of their level of income, personal growth, self-reliance and status in the community. Briefly put, individuals as well as the community realized the benefits of their participation.

The sustainability and viability of the programmes were due to the commitment of the community educators, training of local leaders, the appropriate community entry approach, the typology, the model of community education and the methodologies used in implementing the programmes. Great improvements took place in the lives of beneficiaries of these community education programmes.

www.ingramcontent.com/pod-product-compliance
Lightning Source LLC
Chambersburg PA
CBHW071409290426
44108CB00014B/1754